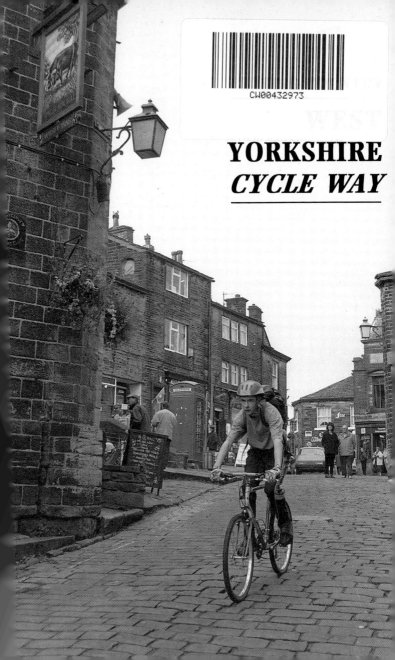

YORKSHIRE
CYCLE WAY

HILLSIDE GUIDES - ACROSS THE NORTH

• •

Long Distance Walks

THE COAST TO COAST WALK	**FURNESS WAY**
DALES WAY COMPANION	**CLEVELAND WAY COMPANION**
THE WESTMORLAND WAY	**THE CUMBERLAND WAY**

NORTH BOWLAND TRAVERSE (David Johnson)
LADY ANNE'S WAY (Sheila Gordon)

Circular Walks - Lancashire
BOWLAND　　**PENDLE & THE RIBBLE**

Circular Walks - Yorkshire Dales
SWALEDALE　　**WENSLEYDALE**
WALKS ON THE HOWGILL FELLS
NIDDERDALE　　**MALHAMDALE**
THREE PEAKS　　**WHARFEDALE**

Circular Walks - North York Moors
BOOK ONE - WESTERN MOORS　　**BOOK THREE - NORTHERN MOORS**
BOOK TWO - SOUTHERN MOORS

Circular Walks - South Pennines
WALKS IN BRONTE COUNTRY　　**WALKS IN CALDERDALE**
ILKLEY MOOR

Circular Walks - North Pennines/Eden
TEESDALE　　**EDEN VALLEY**

Hillwalking - Lake District
OVER LAKELAND MOUNTAINS　　**OVER LAKELAND FELLS**

Yorkshire Pub Walks (Valerie Yewdall)
HARROGATE/WHARFE VALLEY　　**HAWORTH/AIRE VALLEY**

Large format colour hardback
FREEDOM OF THE DALES

BIKING COUNTRY (Richard Peace)
YORKSHIRE DALES CYCLE WAY　　**WEST YORKSHIRE CYCLE WAY**

---

80 DALES WALKS - an omnibus *(published by Cordee, Leicester)*

WALKING COUNTRY TRIVIA QUIZ
Over 1000 questions on the great outdoors

(Books by Paul Hannon unless otherwise stated)

BIKING COUNTRY

WEST YORKSHIRE
CYCLE WAY

Richard Peace

Photographs by
Paul Hannon & Richard Peace

HILLSIDE

HILLSIDE
PUBLICATIONS
11 Nessfield Grove
Keighley
West Yorkshire
BD22 6NU

First published 1995

© Richard Peace 1995

ISBN 1 870141 38 5

Cover illustration: White Wells, Ilkley
Inset: Worth Valley
Back cover: Haworth; Bramham; Sandal Castle
(Paul Hannon/Big Country Picture Library)

Photo credits
Richard Peace: pages 10,37,47,64,67
Paul Hannon: others

Printed in Great Britain by
Fretwell Print And Design
Goulbourne Street
Keighley
West Yorkshire

CONTENTS

WEST YORKSHIRE CYCLE WAY

INTRODUCTION

The West Yorkshire Cycle Way is a 152 mile (245 km) touring route based on a route originally devised by the West Yorkshire Countryside Service, which was part of the now defunct County Council. I have modified it in a few places and spelt this out clearly in the directions where I have done so. Otherwise the route follows the original and is waymarked for much of the way. A very fit cyclist could complete the route in a week but if you want to take it easy and enjoy the scenery then 10 days at least is recommended. The sections can be used as day rides returning by train, but I've also included 6 circular day rides on and around the trail especially for day trippers.

West Yorkshire straddles the hills rolling off the eastern edge of the Pennines and the flat plain onto which they lead. The cycle way reflects this variety and sections are graded 1 to 3 in order of ascending difficulty. Grade 1 is predominantly flat and suitable for beginners and older and younger cyclists. Grade 2 will certainly give even fit cyclists some exercise, whilst grade 3 sections are quite a tough proposition and not really for those without at least some experience (otherwise you'll find yourself pushing your bike uphill a lot).

The human landscape is equally varied from the unkept moors above Holmfirth to Haworth's Bronte Country. The flat, exact pastoral landscape in much of the north-east of the route is in stark contrast to the industrial heritage of the coal field area between Barnsley and Wakefield with its hidden architectural novelties.

IMPORTANT: The waymarking of the white rose on a circular background is accurate and helpful for much of the way, and appears at numerous junctions. However many junctions are not waymarked and it is important to follow the directions accurately. Occasionally the waymarking is WRONG and thus it is especially important to note these instances highlighted in the text.

CYCLING'S BENEFITS

HOW TO HAVE FUN AND STAY HEALTHY AT THE SAME TIME

For newcomers or newly initiated cyclists reading this book who still have any doubt about the benefit of cycling, the following facts may convince you that not only is it enjoyable but highly sensible, especially for those of with even a twinge of a green consciousness:

• Cycling at least 20 miles a week reduces the risk of coronary heart disease to less than half that for non-cyclists. (BUT PLEASE NOTE ALL NON REGULAR TOURING CYCLISTS ARE ADVISED TO CONSULT THEIR DOCTORS BEFORE ATTEMPTING THE CYCLE WAY OR ANY PART OF IT IF THEY HAVE ANY DOUBT ABOUT THEIR HEALTH. THIS IS ESPECIALLY SO IF THEY HAVE A SERIOUS MEDICAL CONDITION).

• Regular cyclists enjoy a fitness level equivalent to being ten years younger than the rest of the population.

• Switching to biking trips as opposed to using motor cars will help international 'ecological' targets to be met, such as the commitment of many nations at the Rio Summit to reducing carbon dioxide emissions to 1990 levels by the year 2000.

• Whatever your personality or age cycling will suit you; I would not advise travelling alone unless experienced but other than this any amount of people can complete the route. If in a large group don't ride several abreast across the road and block traffic coming from behind. This is dangerous.

For details of your local club, which will be a source of information and activities, contact either

Cyclists' Touring Club
Cotterell House, 69 Meadrow, Godalming, Surrey GU17 3HS
(Tel. 01483-417217)

British Cycling Federation
36 Rockingham Road, Kettering, Northants NN16 8HG
(Tel. 01536-412211)

PREPARATION

Safety on the Roads

A few tips to help you enjoy the route safely:

- Always wear a cycle helmet marked with a recognised safety standard
- Use sufficiently bright lights during and after dusk. Spoke reflectors are also important to be seen from the side
- Reflective arm and body bands and bright clothing are a good idea at all times, not just night
- Learn the basic principles of first aid
- Local councils have a selection of safety information and may run safety training courses for absolute beginners
- The condition of brake cables and brake blocks should be checked before every major journey and altered if necessary
- Although rarely seen nowadays I find a rear view mirror fixed onto handlebars very useful. **It should not be used as a substitute for looking over your shoulder to check for traffic coming from behind but as an aid.**
- A horn or bell may be useful to warn pedestrians
- Load the bike equally. Panniers are better than a rucksack which may destabilise you or obscure your rear view.
- Children from one to five years old may be carried in specially designed seats. Between five and ten they should not be allowed on busy roads or unescorted on private ones. They can be accommodated on tandems or purpose built trailers. Local councils run cycling proficiency courses for young children.
- Driving technique: a few pointers for the less experienced
  Build up confidence on quiet lanes
  Avoid swerving for obstacles without checking behind
  See the bicycle section in the highway code
  Signal clearly or get off and cross on foot at busy junctions if you don't feel safe
  Ride positively and confidently to avoid confusing motorists

A wide range of free leaflets with more details on such aspects as lights, helmets and carrying children is available from:
The Bicycle Association, Starley House, Eaton Rd, Coventry CV1 2FH (Tel: 01203-553838)

The Bike

Mountain bike or touring cycle (either can be used to complete the route), the most important factor is to have a cycle that suits your physique, abilities and pocket. The terrain of West Yorkshire is certainly not as challenging as, for example, the Yorkshire Dales where 33% gradients are not uncommon. However there are some steep climbs and a bike with fairly low gearing is still essential. Easy gearing becomes even more important on a gusty day when you're struggling uphill against the wind when you might otherwise be flying up it on a breezeless, warm, sunny day.

Basic maintenance is important and the following are the minimum recommended checks before setting off on each trip:

• Check brake blocks for excessive wear and maintain brake and derailer cables to keep your control of the bike sharp
• Tyres inflated to manufacturer's P.S.I. rating will puncture less easily
• Seat and handlebars should be adjusted to the correct height to feel comfortable and be in control of the bike

Barwick in Elmet

Equipment

Common sense and lightweight compactness is the rule. A basic list that you may wish to add to is set out below.

• Breathable waterproof outers - top and trousers
• Warm and waterproof hat and gloves - the tops of many of the Pennine hills are cold even in summer and the weather on them can change extremely quickly all year round. Wind and rain combined give a windchill factor far exceeding the air temerature which may look quite benign on weather reports.
• Front and rear lights and a rear reflector are legal requirements after dark
• Basic toolkit to include pliers, multi point screwdriver, adjustable spanner and bicycle pump
• Puncture repair kit
• A map and compass are still essential even though you may rely on the maps and directions in the guidebook. The latter should be more than sufficient to get you around the whole of the route but should you happen to take a wrong turn, on top of the moors for example, an Ordnance Survey map will put you back on track. The following Landranger sheets (scale 1:50,000) cover the route, serving each stage as shown: 1 - 104;   2 - 104, 105;   3 - 105, 104
             4 - 105, 111;   5 - 111, 110;   6 - 110, 104
In addition, I found Outdoor Leisure Map 21 - South Pennines (scale 1:25,000) extremely useful on Stages 1 and 6, as the original Cycle Way is shown on it.
Conversions: 1 mile = 1.609 kilometres; 1 metre = 3.2808 feet

Tunnel End, Marsden

Access by Rail

Rail is one of the easiest ways of accessing the route. There are several options; cyclists completing the whole route will obviously only have one point of arrival and departure but for day trippers the circular routes described are based around a train station or if you wish to complete one linear section of the route details are given of the nearest stations for arrival and departure.

There are various rules regarding the carrying of cycles on trains depending on the route, the time and the type of train! It would be a good idea therefore to get hold of the British Rail booklet *Cycling by train* available at most main stations free of charge, which covers the regional railways (enquiries 0151 7019696).

It seems likely the current situation will continue with many longer distance routes requiring a reservation and a £3.00 fee and shorter routes within regional transport executive areas being generally free and on a first come first served basis, subject to peak hour restrictions. Because of the numerous rules and frequent changes to them the only sure fire way is to check with the number above about your particular service.

Note: some stations have relatively steep platform steps that you will have to carry your bike down (e.g. Marsden). Many of the smaller stations are unmanned so you will only be able to get a guard's help as he gets off the train to close the doors - be quick!

Services

Accommodation listings are designed to be 'cyclist friendly'. The following symbols are shorthand for the following facilities:

S = Secure place available to store cycles
D = Facilities available to dry damp clothes
L = Laundry facilities

There is very little available in the way of camping sites on much of the route but anyone prepared to pay £12-£15 per person should easily get bed and breakfast accommodation. Naturally the features in this section change rapidly and are not therefore guaranteed accurate, but rather give an idea of facilities available and comparative prices. Each section concludes listing practical things you might need on the route. The (£) sign next to a bank listing indicates a cashpoint.

21 miles/34km   Grade 2

RAIL ACCESS Haworth (Keighley & Worth Valley Railway)/Ilkley

ROUTE DESCRIPTION

Start the Way by ascending from the bottom of the cobbled main street in Haworth village. **L** *in front of the Tourist Information Centre and* **L** *at the next T-junction onto the main road. Ignore first minor slip left and continue into Stanbury. Through the village on the main road and past Ponden Mill. Past Ponden Reservoir and* **R** *in two-thirds of a mile (s/p Oakworth), continuing on this road to Oakworth in 3 miles. Soon after entering Oakworth* **L** *just after Golden Fleece Inn.* **L** *at first T-junction. At top of small hill* **L** *down Wide Lane (s/p Newsholme). When you meet the cemetery go* **L** *down Slack Lane. Stay on this road ignoring minor turnings, down a dip and over a small stream.*

After 2¼ miles from Oakworth turn **R** *onto Coppy Lane which soon turns into Greystones Lane. Following this road round the head of a small wooded valley (Newsholme Dean) bringing you down Todley Hall Lane to a T-junction and* **R** *into Laycock. Going through the first part of the village look out for a small* **L** *(Chapel Lane) just before a very ornate graveyard. If you see a war memorial plaque on the wall to your left you have just gone too far! Climb this small lane to a T-junction and* **R** *to a further T-junction facing Redcar Tarn, going* **L** *(s/p Steeton). Follow this road for 3 miles into Steeton as it descends steeply through Whitley Head.*

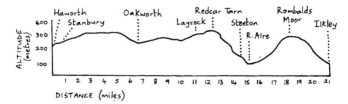

*Coming into Steeton proper look for a wall post box on the left and turn **L** into Mill Lane, seeing a church spire straight ahead of you. At the T-junction past the green on the right, turn **R** bringing you to crossroads. Go **L** for the train station (by the Goat's Head and Old Star pubs). Descend to roundabout crossing over the A629 and onto A6034, over river Aire. In just over a mile, through the start of Silsden, go over the canal bridge and first **R** just over it. Through suburbia to a **L** by cemetery, then first **R** through Brunthwaite.*

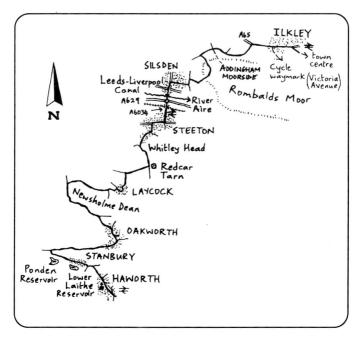

*After ascending (steeply in places) for just over 2 miles, and going past two bridleways, hit a T-junction opposite a farm and go **R**. A lovely descent of about 2½ miles brings you to the A65 (at previous fork go **R** on more main road a little before hitting A65). Go **R** onto the A65. Look for waymarked **R** onto Victoria Avenue after 40 mph signs coming into Ilkley. This takes you into the town centre on the route of the Cycle Way itself.*

• **Haworth** The main street is a suitably picturesque place to start and finish the route. The steep, cobbled street is flanked by a brooding church and merrier clusters of old shop buildings. Most famous as the home of the Bronte sisters, you can learn all you wish to about this literary family at the Bronte Parsonage Museum, a Georgian residence containing relics of the Bronte family who inhabited it. (01535 642323 £3.60 - concessions for senior citizens, students, and UB40s. Open 10-5 April-September, 11-4.30 October-March. Closed Christmas, and January 10-February 4).

The Parish church at the top of the main street dates from the demolition of the old church in 1879 and contains the family tomb of the Brontes (only Anne is not buried here; she lies at Scarborough). The Bronte memorial chapel within also has interesting documents telling part of the story of the Brontes' lives. In the graveyard look for the tombstone of Lily Cove, Britain's first balloonist and parachutist. Her death contained elements of farce and irony as the brave pioneer became detached from her parachute during a 1906 exhibition! Also look out for Haworth Old Hall just off the bottom of the main street, a stone clad Tudor building.

St. Michael's, Haworth

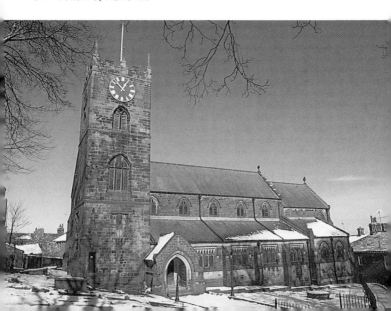

• The Keighley and Worth Valley Railway has a station at Haworth. For full details see Stage 6 and details of Oxenhope, where the railway begins.

• Stanbury church contains the top layer of the three decker pulpit used by Reverend Bronte at the original church at Haworth.

• There is very natural moorland separating Haworth from Steeton and Silsden and an equally beautiful section cutting over the western corner of Rombalds Moor (the famed Ilkley Moor is part of this, being the smaller moor rising to the south of Ilkley).

• Nationally famous for being the place of the invention of the 'Yorkshire National Anthem' *On Ilkley Moor Baht'at,* **Ilkley** is not at all in keeping with the thick Dales accents in which the song is often repeated, but ironically its a markedly upper middle class residential town, crammed with intricate Victorian architecture. It lies on the gradient that rises gradually from the Wharfe and joins the foot of the moor where gradients steepen dramatically. It is well worth spending at least half a day in and around the town. Ilkley town centre and its surroundings are full of interesting sights as shown on the accompanying map. In addition, look out for the following within walking distance of the town centre.

• **White Wells** Possibly the town's most distinctive visitor attraction. Visible from various parts of the town centre near the river these former open air baths sit commandingly on the slopes of Ilkley Moor. A local squire first exploited the local resource in the mid 1700's and a hydropathic company later added roofs and various other extensions. The baths are now a museum.

• **Cow and Calf Rocks** The Cycle Way passes next to these famous local features ascending Hangingstone Road (after Cowpasture Road). The unmistakable larger 'Cow' rock has a sheer 50ft rock face and its smaller offspring is easily recognisable close by.

• **The Swastika Stone** Possibly Yorkshire's oldest rock carving this has nothing to do with Nazism, with which the sign is most often associated, but rather pre-Celtic civilisations. It is accessed from Heber's Ghyll, a picturesque local beauty spot. A footpath leads up the small wooded valley, off Heber's Ghyll Drive.

A LOOK AROUND ILKLEY

1 *St Margaret's Church* This luxurious new church was opened in 1879 because of overcrowding at the existing church. Designed by famous architect Norman Shaw.

2 *Wells House* - Bradford and Ilkley Community College. Originally a 'hydropathic' - open to paying guests. Its Italianate style reflects the continental origins of the supposed magic water treatment.

3 *Deaconess Court* - Old Ilkley College. Originally a school, it was later used as a place to train deaconesses.

4 *Parish Ghyll Road* Crammed with typical, wealthy middle-class Victorian residences, it reflects the wealth attracted to the town in the latter part of the nineteenth century.

5 *Convalescent Hospital* Built in Scottish style, originally to provide 'water treatment' for people who could not afford to pay.

6 *Canker Well* Look for a stone bath near the well in this public garden. Originally there was a natural spring where people came to drink or splash water externally: it has dried up due to subsequent development. The stone bath is inscribed with a dedication to Vincent Priessnitz, founder of hydropathy.

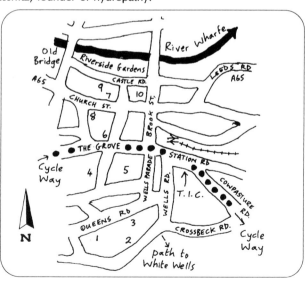

7 *Manor House Museum* 16th/17th century house converted to a museum and art gallery including yeoman farmer's house, historical display and artist's/craftsmen's gallery.

8 *Victorian Arcade* Built in 1894 and recently reconstructed in the original style.

9 *Donkey Jackson's Steps* Stone steps leading up to allotments: they are the remainder of a donkey hiring business which visitors used to get to White Wells.

10 *All Saints Church* features 'the saxon crosses' blending pagan and christian traditions.

The old packhorse bridge just before the golf course links to the Riverside gardens and was built around 1675. It marked the traditional fording point of the river on the Roman road to Boroughbridge.

The Old Bridge, Ilkley

Stanbury across the Worth Valley

Accommodation

Cobwebs Guesthouse, 11 West Lane **Haworth**   01535 64250
£17.50 (evening meal £10)

Apothecary Guest House, 86 Main Street **Haworth**   01535 643642
£18.50 (tea rooms with meals until 5.30)   Facilities: S

There are numerous guest houses at the bottom of the cobbled main street.
You should get a room out of peak season here easily.

Osborne House, 1 Tivoli Place **Ilkley** 01943 609483   £14   Facilities: S

Glengarth, 3 Grange Estate **Ilkley**   01943 609372   £18   Facilities: S;D

Mrs. Roberts, 63 Skipton Road **Ilkley** 01943 817542   £16   Facilities: S;D

Belvedere, 2 Victoria Avenue **Ilkley** 01943 607598   £13   Facilities: S;D

Food

Old White Lion Hotel, Main Street **Haworth**
Bar snacks from £1.40 and restaurant meals up to £11
Beers: Websters Yorkshire, Wilsons Original, John Smiths

Old Silent Inn **Stanbury**
Meals from £1.50   Beers: Theakstons, Youngers

18

Wuthering Heights Inn Stanbury
Meals £3-£3.50   Beers: Taylors, Tetleys

Friendly Inn Stanbury
Meals and snacks under £5
Beers: Tetleys, Burton Ale, Wild Boar, guest beers
Closed Tuesday lunchtimes in Winter

Grouse Inn Oakworth
A more up-market establishment with meals over £6   Beers: Taylors

Betty's, The Grove Ilkley
Fine tea house. Snacks and drink would be over £5. An unusually quaint and
rarefied atmosphere. Not really recommended if you're in full bike gear!

There are also a couple of cafes at the bottom of Brook Street before you hit
the main Leeds Road.

Camping

Old Silent Inn **Stanbury** Facilities unknown, enquire for further details

Upper Heights Farm **Stanbury** Mr. & Mrs. Baxter 01535 644592

Silsden The following sites are within a couple of miles of the route, to the
north-west of Silsden. Ring for accurate directions from Silsden.

Dales Bank Holiday Park, off Bradley Road
£5.50 per tent; showers, H&C water, WC, showers, clubhouse
Open April-October 01535 653321

Lower Heights Farm
£1.50 per tent; WC only. Cheap and basic!
Open Easter-October 01535 653035

Mrs. Mason, Maynard Ing, Cocking Lane **Addingham Moorside**
01943 830396 (see map for location)

Tourist Information
2-4 West Lane **Haworth** 01535 642329
Station Road **Ilkley** 01943 602319

Banks
Natwest, 19 The Grove **Ilkley** (£)
Midland, 1 Wells Road **Ilkley** (£)

Natwest, 59 Kirkgate **Silsden**
Barclays, 9 Brook Street **Ilkley** (£)
Lloyds, 29 Brook Street **Ilkley** (£)

Cycle shops
Robin Nolan Cycles, 153 Oakworth Road, **Keighley** 01535 667829
Riley Brothers, 12 James Avenue, Eastburn, **Steeton** 01535 652166
Wharfedale Cycles, 32 Leeds Road, **Ilkley** 01943 607957
ID's Bicycle workshop, 42a Nelson Road, **Ilkley** 01943 816101

CIRCULAR ROUTE

BEAMSLEY AND LANGBAR MOOR

12 miles/19km   **A hard grade 2**

The most obvious route based on Ilkley is the circuit of the
roads around the edge of Rombalds Moor, but this lesser known
and shorter alternative on the opposite side of the valley takes
a smaller, quieter and wilder road. At first the road clings lazily
to the side of the valley giving you good views of Addingham,
but the initial gentle gradients give no warning of the steep and
spectacular ascent which lies ahead after the route doubles
back on itself through the sleepy village of Beamsley. The 'jewel
in the crown' of this lovely ascent is a stunning 180 degree-plus
panorama of the surrounding moors from the hamlet of Langbar,
which represents the highest point of the ride.

You can relax after your hard work on the climb as the road
threads past farms on the upper northern slopes of the Wharfe
Valley, dropping gradually back and entering Ilkley via Ben
Rhydding. If you have accessed the route by train you may cut
your journey short and get back on the line at Ben Rhydding
station, the penultimate stop on the Leeds - Ilkley line. Note that
outside of Ilkley there are
no eating or drinking
places so take your own
supplies if you want to
make this a long and lei-
surely ride. A relatively
short route but one to
take slowly and savour.

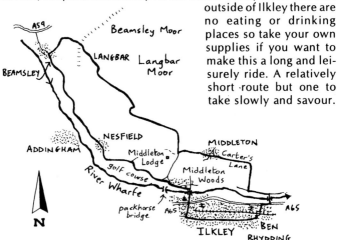

Start the ride on Station Road outside Ilkley station, heading right towards the town centre. Turn **R** downhill at the next junction onto Brook Street. Cross over the main A65 Leeds-Skipton road and over the main river bridge. First **L** leads into the quiet suburbia of Denton Road (Middleton Lodge 1 mile), going past a packhorse bridge on the left and continuing through a golf course as the road turns into Nesfield Road.

The road hugs the valley bottom as you continue past Addingham on the opposite side of the valley. After going through the cluster of houses at Nesfield continue into Beamsley and take the first **R** (Langbar 1¾). A first steep climb leads round a bend and a second extended and steeper climb brings you to the tiny settlement of Langbar on Langbar Moor.

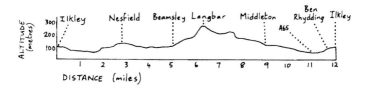

21

At the end of Langbar the road you follow twists right and a private road and footpath carries straight on. After a freewheeling descent off Middleton Moor look out for a **L** (s/p Middleton and Ilkley).

Going through Middleton go straight over the crossroads onto Carter's Lane and descend to a T-junction going **L** then first **R** over a small bridge. **R** on hitting the A65 main road and straight away slip **L** on a 'B' road which will bring you uphill and under a railway bridge to Ben Rhydding station on the right. This road leads through this highly desirable suburb back onto Station Road and to your starting point.

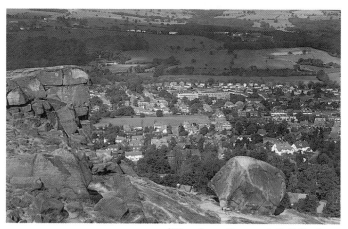

Ilkley from Cow and Calf Rocks

ALONG THE WAY

• The stretch of the route after Nesfield gives good views of the church at Addingham.

• There are spectacular panoramas all the way up Langbar and Middleton moors, especially to the north-west to the moors that close in on Bolton Abbey ruins.

• On the descent to Middleton before turning onto the road across the valley you might like to sample the Stations of the Cross walk in the grounds of Middleton Lodge, itself a Catholic retreat.

LIVING HISTORY AT ILKLEY

The typical Victorian spa town

In contrast to the heavy industrial areas that predominate in West Yorkshire, Ilkley has always been a retreat of the 'better off'. Strictly a town of middle class values it boasts elegant buildings against the dramatic backdrop of Ilkley Moor.

The healing properties of its natural waters began to attract attention in the early 1800's and the town became a practicable commuter settlement in the 1860's with the provision of a railway link to Leeds. Cultural refinement, fresh air and supposedly curative waters were all within easy travelling distance of the workplace.

To today's mind the treatment of illnesses and ailments with something as simple as water may seem puzzling, however what started as a local industry, which grew by word of mouth, was put on a soundly scientific footing in 1844 with the opening of the first 'hydropathic', the Ben Rhydding - an ornate palatial masterpiece of Victorian design.

What would pass for torture now was then respected therapy affordable only by the rich; a regime including cold baths, brisk air and plain food may seem pointlessly dour today but attracted enough 'clients' in the mid and late nineteenth century to create more than one fortune for the promoters of the 'Ilkley cure.'

However popular belief in such cures as 'the cold douche' and the 'plunge bath' (both using cold water) waned and the decline of the Ilkley hydropaths in the late nineteenth century was compounded by two instances of national scandal involving once highly regarded proponents of the cure. One practitioner was involved in a sensational murder case whilst an even more dubious individual pronounced one of his patients dead whilst undergoing the doctors' own hydrotherapy treatment (whilst being wrapped in a blanket soaked in cold water). A subsequent doctor revived the unlucky child from his unconscious state with warm blankets and milk.

• Middleton Woods are predominantly oak and sycamore woods. Some 90 acres of woodland make a pleasant stroll and contain an old stone bridge and 'Jacob's Ladder' steps (from the biblical steps leading to heaven).

STAGE TWO

ILKLEY TO WETHERBY

23 miles/37km   **Fairly easy grade 2 after a grade 3 climb**

RAIL ACCESS Ilkley/Cattal (10km north on Knaresborough-York line)

RAIL ACCESS Ilkley/Cattal (10km north on Knaresborough-York line)

ROUTE DESCRIPTION

Continue up Victoria Avenue after entering Ilkley (Stage 1 describes the approach on the A65 after descending from Rombalds Moor). Over two sets of minor crossroads go L on meeting Grove Road, bringing you to a T-junction with the main street (The Grove). Follow this road past the church with the distinctively tall spire on the right, and past the station look for the R up Cowpasture Road (Cow and Calf Rocks 1m). The road climbs steeply out of Ilkley, past the Cow and Calf Rocks on the right, then the hotel of the same name on the left.

*In just under 3 miles pass through the village of Burley Woodhead and shortly after L (s/p Menston) on Moor Lane. **Note:** do not confuse this with a left turning for Menston down another Moor Lane as you are entering Burley Woodhead; make sure you have gone past the Hermit Inn before you make the correct turn down the second Moor Lane.*

The Chevin you are about to climb rises up in front of you. Staying on the main road through Menston curve right then left by the recreation ground, coming to the A65 and going straight across (Buckle Lane). On meeting the Chevin End pub bear R at this junction of four roads (not most immediate right). You'll know you are on the right road if you are running parallel with a string of power lines on the left. Shortly take a L at the next T-junction then immediate R.

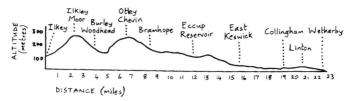

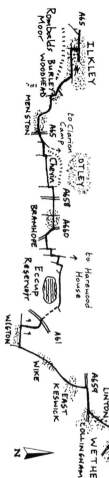

Go along the top of Guiseley Moor and the Chevin. Coming to the next T-junction go **L** then immediate **R** which road leads you straight across the A658 to the old centre of Bramhope village, going straight across the road by the market cross.

Coming to the A660 **R** onto this main road then third left down a minor road (s/p Eccup). At the next set of junctions go **L** then immediate **R**. Wend your way **L** at the next T-junction then **R** in a small dip, **R** at the next T-junction and **L** at the next fork. Pass the dead end sign, through 'no entry' signs and above the north shore of Eccup Reservoir. Approaching treatment works turn **R** onto grass bridleway (don't go over the cattle grid). Rejoin a tarmac road and go **R** which takes you right next to the eastern end of Eccup Reservoir.

Follow this road away from the reservoir and through woods. Rejoin A61 and cross straight over onto poorly metalled road. Follow this to a T-junction (watch out just before the junction; the road crosses the tee-off area of a golf course). **L** at this junction through a modern residential area and **L** at next T-junction. Continue on this road for just over 4 miles, through Wike village and East Keswick to T-junction with the A659, going **R**.

Half a mile after coming into Collingham take a slip road **L** (s/p Linton) and continue over a bridge and up a small hill into this village. **R** at the next T-junction (s/p Wetherby). At next T-junction with A661 go **R** into Wetherby and in 70 yards **L** down Crossley Street to T-junction in front of the mail delivery office and **L** here (right will take you into the town centre). Continue on this main road and just before an Esso garage and opposite a telephone box **R** onto York road. This road continues over the A1 towards a racecourse.

• Climbing out of Ilkley there are stupendous views over the river Wharfe and beyond. Passing through the quiet village of Burley Woodhead and turning towards the suburbia of Menston you get a good idea of the unusual ridge topography of Guiseley Moor leading up to the Chevin Ridge. Once on the ridge you should be able to look out over the Leeds/Bradford airport at Yeadon. It is easy to cycle past one of the best views on this ride, that from the Chevin over the Wharfe Valley. Just before the Royalty Inn turn left into the Beacon House car park and take in the majestic view. There is a useful map showing local bridleways and the way to the White House visitor centre and tea room.

• The old centre of **Bramhope** has something of the feeling of a miniaturised staging post about it; a distinctive market cross and lantern mark the centre.

• **Harewood House** Off route just before Eccup Reservoir. Designed by the renowned John Carr in 1759, with equally exquisite Robert Adam interior, this former home of HRH Princess Mary contains both Chippendale furniture and masterpieces of Italian painting. It also has a famous bird garden and Capability Brown landscaped gardens. Open March-Nov, daily 11-5.

Bramhope

26

• **Wetherby** The market town of Wetherby lacks the dramatic moorland backdrop of Ilkley and Victorian extravagance of its architecture, but what it lacks it grandeur it makes up for with the homely small scale nature of the town centre and the feeling that it is still a 'locals' village'. This is despite the onset of twentieth century suburbia and the widening of the main street to accommodate large volumes of traffic.

The whole of the village was once owned by the Duke of Devonshire until it was sold in individual lots in 1824. Market town and staging post, herds of cows were once a common sight being driven down the high street, flanked by pens containing sheep and pigs (the holdfasts can still be seen periodically down the side of the High Street). You can take in the main features of the centre with the map and guide overleaf.

By the Wharfe at Wetherby Bridge

A LOOK ROUND WETHERBY

1 *Catholic church* Built in 1986 the architecture clearly reflects the constraints of the small space available.

2 *Methodist chapel* The present building was built in 1829 and the site was the basis of the Wesleyan faith that predominated amongst the local traders and craftsmen.

3 *St. James' church* Built from local subscriptions in the mid nineteenth century.

4 *Swan & Talbot Inn* Both this and the Angel were the basis of the local economy when Wetherby was primarily a staging post between London and Edinburgh. At one time the tenants of both inns combined owned more than 460 acres and had facilities to stable 170 horses.

5 *The Angel Inn*

6 *The Shambles* Originally a row of butchers' shops built by local patron the Duke of Devonshire. The facade was added in the 19th century.

7 *Town Hall* Again funded by local subscription this building has had many uses since its construction in 19th century, from county court to local dance hall, acting as the focal point for a small community.

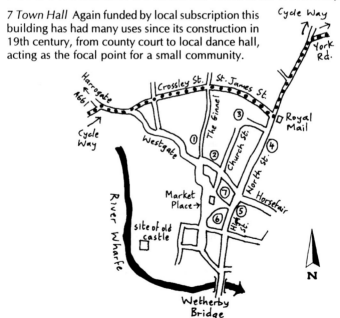

The Hermit Inn, Burley Woodhead

Accommodation

Glendales, Muddy Lane **Linton** 01937 892530

Food

There are cafes at the Ilkley nurseries and at the White House centre on the Chevin (see map for location details)

Chevin Inn, Chevin End **Menston**
Meals: £3-£9
Beers: John Smiths, Magnet, Courage Directors

Royalty Inn, York Gate **Otley Chevin**
Snacks and meals from £1.55
Beers: Tetleys, guest beer

Bramhope boasts a fish and chip shop and restaurant serving less usual items such as salmon.

George and Dragon **Wetherby** (at end of High Street by the river)
Cheap meals and snacks from £2
Beers: John Smiths
Open all lunchtimes throughout the year. 'Lock up facilities for cyclists'.
Catering for large groups.

Camping
Clarion Camp, Chevin Road, **Menston** 01924 382952
(approaching the Chevin pub bear left and site is on the right in a short while)
£2 per tent. WC, showers   Open April-October

Royalty Inn, York Gate **Otley Chevin** 01943 461156

Wetherby Racecourse Caravan Club **Wetherby** 01937 582035
Showers, WC.
Open early June-mid September (when the racing season has finished - the club actually uses part of the course)

Tourist Information
Council Offices, 8 Boroughgate **Otley** 01943 465151
Council Offices, 24 Westgate **Wetherby** 01937 582706

Banks

Otley	**Wetherby**
Midland, 25 Crossgates (£)	Natwest, 49 High Street (£)
Natwest, 7 Manor Square (£)	Midland, 11 North Street (£)
Barclays, 2 Manor Square (£)	Barclays, 26 Market Place (£)

Cycle shops
Chevin Cycles, Gay Lane **Otley** 01943 462773
Wheels in Motion, 21 High Street **Wetherby** 01937 588228

Wharfedale from Otley Chevin

WETHERBY TO CASTLEFORD

21 miles/34km   **Grade 1**

RAIL ACCESS Cattal/Castleford

ROUTE DESCRIPTION

*Continuing on from Stage 2 exit Wetherby crossing over the A1 and in a third of a mile take the signed bridleway off the B1224 just after the main entrance to the racecourse. Over the tarmac and climb over the road (part unsurfaced) passing racecourse buildings until you get to T-junction and go **L**. At the next small crossroads go **R** (s/p Boston Spa) and continue into Thorp Arch. Continue through the village past the pub on the right and down over the river (to visit the church take the small left before the war memorial). Crossing the river brings you to the main road in Boston Spa, going **R** on A659 into centre and **L** down Church Lane immediately past the Crown Hotel.*

*Soon arriving in Clifford turn **L** on hitting main road by church and immediate **R** taking you onto quiet country lane (Old Mill Lane). Past a disused windmill tower on your left coming into Bramham. At T-junction ignore left for Tadcaster and after **R** here go second **R**, (s/p Bramham 1¼) onto the High Street and down hill past Swan pub. Arrive at the war memorial with Red Lion pub on the right and turn **L** going through the village to a T-junction and **R**. Next **L** takes you over A1, continuing on this road past a right for Wothersome, and past Bramham Hall, until you come to a bridleway on the left after nearly 3 miles (waymarked off a right-hand bend and leading behind some woods, but otherwise easy to miss). After going **L** down here continue to junction with A64 (beware very muddy at end - used by tractors) going **L** then very shortly first **R** down a minor road.*

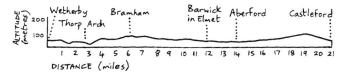

31

Through small settlement of Potterton and **L** at next major junction, bringing you into Barwick in Elmet. On entering Barwick in Elmet swing **L** in front of the church and down the road signposted for Aberford. Follow this road into Aberford to T-junction and **R** up the main street, passing Swan Hotel and church on the right. Carry on out of the village past the beautiful almshouses on the right. (Alternative route - via Lotherton Hall: further up the main street take the **L** (s/p Lotherton Hall.)

After visiting Lotherton Hall pick up the B1217 back to junction with A656 for Castleford after passing under the A1).

If not visiting Lotherton Hall carry on out of Aberford to next major road junction and go straight across onto the A656 for Castleford. Carry on this road for nearly 4 miles, going through a roundabout and past Ledston Luck business park and **L** at the next crossroads for Ledsham. The imposing Ledston Hall comes into view on your right and then take first **R** (s/p Ledston) taking you through Ledston village to a T-junction.

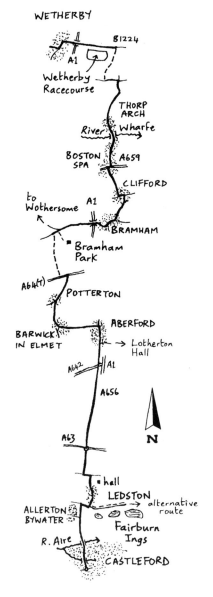

*At this T-junction the original route is waymarked right. However there is a very interesting scenic detour via the RSPB reserve of Fairburn Ings, which involves a short walk on a footpath through the reserve and a short carry up steep steps over a railway. You should be able to carry your bike on one shoulder and use the other hand on the guide rail to do this safely. If you want to do this latter route go **L** at this junction. If you don't fancy this, pick up the original route through Castleford town centre; both routes are described in Stage 4.*

ALONG THE WAY

• Thorp Arch, Boston Spa and Clifford are a string of pleasant villages on the flat lands around the lower Wharfe linked in character by the local magnesium limestone from which many of their buildings are constructed.

The main road through **Thorp Arch** descends to good views over the Wharfe and views of handsome woods above a weir. The village church is a little way out of the village but worth a quick detour (see directions). Rising away from the Wharfe brings you to the A659 running through **Boston Spa**. Inhabitants of this village must have thought they had really put themselves on the map when in the late 18th century the town began to attract visitors who came to take hydropathic treatment in its natural waters. However the wealth and growth anticipated did not materialise and much of this lucrative trade went to nearby Harrogate. This was due partly, no doubt, to Queen Victoria's preferential treatment of Boston Spa's northern neighbour.

The most unusual and main attraction of **Clifford** is its distinctive and continental looking Catholic church; unmissable as you come onto the main street and turn left next to it. The village has strong historical ties with the Catholic faith and nearby Clifford Moor was the rallying point for local Catholic forces during the Rising of the North in 1569 and also in the Civil War. It is easy to see where the strong continental influence comes from in the church's architecture when you realise that it counted the Duke of Parma, the King of Sardinia and the Queen of France amongst its benefactors.

• **Bramham Park** Sumptuous Queen Anne mansion amidst continental style gardens. Open 19th June-4th Sept, 9.15-5.30, Tues, Wed, Thur, Sun and bank holiday weekend.

CIRCULAR ROUTE

ABERFORD AND THE VILLAGES OF THE PLAIN OF YORK

22 miles/36km   **Grade 1**

The flat plain of York makes for relatively easy cycling country (unless there is a strong westerly wind which really picks up speed over these large flat tracts and can stop you dead in your tracks). Garforth provides rail access but the real 'stars' of this route are the villages dotted around the huge intensively farmed fields south of York. Although Lotherton Hall is the major focal point for tourists in the area, the beautiful old brick architecture of villages such as Church Fenton could claim top billing on this ride. This gloriously vernacular architecture combines with several stylish pubs which provide ample opportunity for 'fuelling up'.

*From the train station in Garforth turn **R** onto the main road (the A642). Follow this for just over 2 miles and immediately before the slip road onto the A1 take the **L** signposted for Aberford. Coming past the beautifully elaborate Almshouses on the left brings you into the village and first **R** down Lotherton Lane (s/p Lotherton Hall & Sherburn). At the T-junction opposite the entrance to Lotherton Hall **L** then first **R** (s/p Sherburn in Elmet) taking you gently downhill. Take the next **L**. At the T-junction on entering Saxton, opposite the Plough pub, **R** takes you towards Barkston Ash (left takes you into the village itself and the atmospheric Greyhound pub next to the church).*

*On meeting the A162 go **R** then after two small turnings left take the third **L** (s/p Church Fenton and Ryther. A **L** down a private road (s/p to a Catholic church) takes you past a small lake to the church (access to the church only, no thoroughfare). If you want to explore this avenue you will have to turn round and backtrack to the main road*

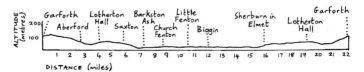

34

through the village. The road then heads straight into Church Fenton over the railway bridge and the delightful station-cum-restaurant. In the village take the *R* at the White Horse pub (s/p Sherburn in Elmet) going past the church on the left. After coming into the countryside take the next *L* which takes you straight through the charming Little Fenton, and onto a T-junction in Biggin, going *R* here.

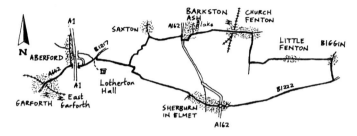

You are now on the 'return journey' and on meeting the B1222 go *R* and after a longish stretch of road go through two roundabouts and uphill to the centre of Sherburn in Elmet. Go straight over the main junction at the top of the hill (right is s/p A162 for Tadcaster). Just as the church comes into view take the *R*, marked as Sir John's Lane. Follow this lane, generally gently uphill, back to the junction with the B1217 at Lotherton Hall, going *L* here. Meeting the A642 at the next T-junction go *L* onto it and under the A1. This directs you back into Garforth and past the train station on the left. If you have chosen to start from Aberford go *R* to it just under the A1 bridge.

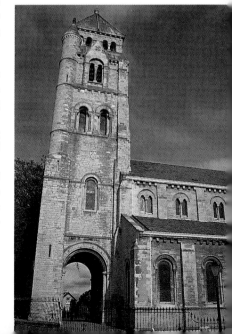

St. Edward's Roman Catholic church, Clifford

• **Lotherton Hall** You pass near Lotherton Hall twice, once on the way out and coming back so you could break your journey here whenever suits you. This Edwardian aristocratic home has a host of attractions, including one of the largest bird gardens in the country. The house itself contains art, furniture and costumes. Hall and gardens are open Tues-Sun 10.30-12.00, 1.00-5.30 (closed Mondays except bank holidays). There is also a restaurant. There are good walks around the estate woodlands and Coburn Hill Woods.

• **Aberford** village sits picturesquely astride a beck and has a number of pleasant village pubs. It is different from most of the villages you go on to visit afterwards whose brick architecture contrasts strikingly with the local limestone used in Aberford.

• There are numerous small scale attractions in the rest of the villages. The Greyhound pub in Saxton and the railway/restaurant building in Church Fenton are possibly the most interesting, but there are many others.

The Greyhound, Saxton

The Wharfe between Thorp Arch and Boston Spa

SERVICES

Accommodation

Lomond Lodge, The Close **Boston Spa** 01937 842588
£16
Facilities: S;D

Lincliffgarth, 5 Fountains Avenue **Boston Spa** 01937 844049
£16

Meals

The Red Lion, The Square **Bramham** (En route in town centre).
Meals averaging £4.50
Beers: Sam Smiths

Banks **Boston Spa**	Barclays, 160b High Street
	Midland, 117 High Street
	Natwest, 187 High Street

Cycle shops
Sherburn Cycle Centre, 14a Finkle Hill **Sherburn in Elmet** 01977 683425

16 miles/26km   Grade 1

RAIL ACCESS Castleford/Fitzwilliam, Moorthorpe or South Elmsall

ROUTE DESCRIPTION

There are two alternative routes; Fairburn Ings avoids the busy
Castleford town centre but involves a push along a footpath and a
carry over steep steps on the side of a railway bridge.

1. Via Fairburn Ings
On coming to the T-junction after Ledston, **L** *brings you onto a nice
long stretch of road past various water filled coal pits known as
Fairburn Ings, which are now an RSPB protected bird reserve. Follow
this road into Fairburn village noticing the ruins of an abbey protruding from the water in one of the ings, about halfway to the village. On
coming into Fairburn look for the second right which goes through a
small car park and continues through a no access sign. When the road
becomes unmetalled dismount as you are now on a footpath.
Continue through the nature reserve to the end of the path and go* **L**.
*Still walking go over the canal bridge in the form of two lock gates and
under the railway bridge, carrying your bike over the river at the far
side. and following the railway for a short while.*

*Remount on bending left by sewage works. Coming to a gate on the
left, go through it and* **R** *at the unmetalled crossroads towards the
housing estate (Castleford's Water Fryston estate). Join the metalled
road carrying straight on through the estate and ignoring small left
turns until going uphill you see Kestrel Drive and go* **L** *down it. Follow*

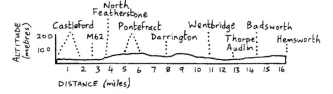

38

this road until you hit Hillcrest Mount jinking **L** then **R**, staying on Hillcrest Mount and going over speed ramps. At the T-junction at the end of Hillcrest Mount go **L** onto the B6136 heading towards Ferrybridge C power station. Before coming to the power station look for a small farm track on the **R**, opposite Holmfield Nurseries (you've gone too far if you start to pass the power station). This unmetalled track takes you across the M62 and continues to join the back of Nevison housing estate in Pontefract. Carry on this road through the estate and at next two T-junctions go **L** then **R** respectively. This road goes under a railway bridge; follow it uphill and as it bends left to the next T-junction which brings you to the back of the castle. Go **R** and uphill taking first **L** up a one way street and **L** at the end bringing you to the castle entrance. Rejoin the main route by going away from the castle entrance down Micklegate, and **L** at the end.

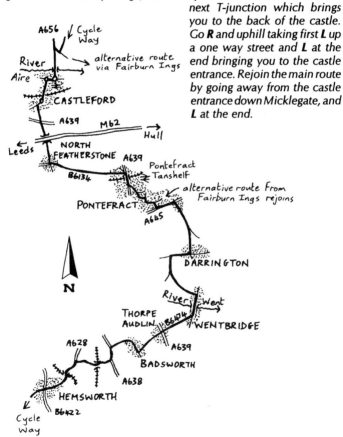

39

2. The original Cycle Way through Castleford town centre

On reaching the T-junction after Ledston village turn **R** as waymarked. On meeting the A656 go **L** and continue on this road to a roundabout at the start of Castleford town centre just after bridge; go **R** here. At next roundabout go **L** (s/p Normanton & Featherstone). Past the Parish church on the right and down a shop-lined street, past bus station on the left. Straight over the next roundabout and over a level crossing, then up a hill and shortly after the Commercial Hotel go **L** into Aketon Road. Carry on past the William IV pub and over the A639 and under the M62.

Note: there may be a new junction in the near future about a third of a mile before passing under the M62, so be aware that you will want to continue on this road and not take the new road. Pass through open countryside and shortly after entering North Featherstone meet the B6134 and go **L** (Park Lane). Go past the New College on the left and meet the A639 going **R** (Just before this junction there is a left into Pontefract Park which has a racecourse and boating lake).

Shortly after going past Pontefract Tanshelf railway station go **L** down Stuart Rd and **R** just before Morrisons supermarket taking you past Tescos on the right and a swimming pool on the left. At the next T-junction go **R** s/p for the castle and waymarked. Follow the road as it curves left in front of the Town Hall and goes down Horsefair, past the Woodmans Inn on the right and comes to a T-junction with traffic lights. Go **L** here and then in 300 yards there will be a **R** on Baghill Lane (s/p Darrington). Leading out of Pontefract turn **R** at the first fork (sign shows no access to lorries over 7.5 tons). This brings you into Darrington, going **R** at the first crossroads then first **L** (s/p East Hardwick & Wentbridge). Going down this lane ignore the first right for East Hardwick (there should be an ice cream cone shaped water tower ahead of you in the distance as a landmark).

Coming into Wentbridge go **R** at the first T-junction and past the Wentbridge House Hotel on the left and over a river. Just after the corner shop B&B go **R** (s/p Thorpe Audlin). Follow this road (B6474) to a crossroads and across the A639. Through the village of Thorpe Audlin to a mini-roundabout on the edge of Badsworth. **R** here and past the church on the right. Shortly after exiting the village go **L** when you hit the A638 and immediate **R** (s/p Hemsworth). Continue on Royd Moor Lane to T-junction with the A628 and **L** bringing you into Hemsworth. At the first major junction by the church continue out of Hemsworth on the A628 for Barnsley.

• **Castleford & Fairburn Ings** You would hardly expect to find a bird sanctuary of major importance right next to a town famed before recession for being at the heartland of industry and especially mining, but if you take the alternative route through Fairburn Ings this is exactly where you find yourself. Famous for the numerous species of waterfowl, this area of shallow water filled coal excavations is now a protected RSPB reserve. If you want to see a number of the commoner species close to, the best place to observe them is the small layby on the main road on your right adjoining the main expanse of water.

Shortly before this, on a bend above a smaller area of water, look out for the ruins of an old abbey bathing in the water that have become rich feeding grounds for so many birds. The 'walk and carry' section through the reserve leads you through a more natural habitat of ings surrounded by tree cover where you will have to be quieter and look harder, but the reward may be a sight of a few rarer species. Even if you've no ornithological interest whatsoever I still think it is a pleasanter route than going through Castleford town centre.

• **Wentbridge and Darrington** Of these two cosy villages Wentbridge has more charm, partly due to its natural location at the head of the river Went, and its smattering of shops and restaurants and pubs has not been invaded by that modern disease, terminal suburbia. On the road after going right in Darrington the next left for East Hardwick and Wentbridge will bring you to a modern house called *Mannaseh* set back in its own grounds. It may look innocuous enough but it was designed by its former owner, John Poulson. Those old enough will remember the infamous corruption scandal surrounding this architect who 'bought' government contracts in an affair that lead to ministerial resignation.

• **Pontefract** Now continuing in the mining tradition of Castleford, Pontefract was once a centre for liquorice growing and liquorice fields were a common sight here (honestly). All types of sweets were derived from this crop. Nowadays the main attraction for the visitor is the ruins of Pontefract Castle perched domineeringly above on a natural rise at the centre of the town.

Pontefract Museum has displays centring on the castle and an early priory. Housed in Art Noveau building. Mon-Sat 10.30 -5.00, Sun 2.30-5.00.

41

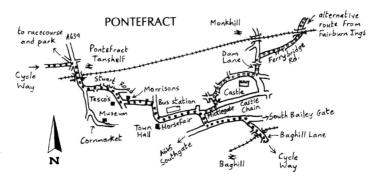

SERVICES

Accommodation

Mr. I. Goodworth, The Corner Cafe, **Wentbridge** 01977 620316
£16 Facilities: S

Bridge End Guest House, Great North Road, **Wentbridge** 01977 620314
£18-£20

Visset Cottage Hotel, Barnsley Road **Hemsworth** 01977 610765
(on left whilst exiting village on cycle route)
£19.50 (double - £32.50)   Facilities: S;D;L   Food: Starters from £1.95
Camping from £4 per night

Food

Spread Eagle **Darrington**
Traditional food and daily specials £1.95-£13.50   Beers: Stones, Bass

Swiss Cottage Restaurant **Wentbridge**
(coming to the T-junction into Wentbridge go left instead of right)
Meals around £5

Wentbridge House Hotel **Wentbridge**
Fine French cuisine. One of the very finest restaurants in the area. Only go
here if you have very deep pockets and preferably not in your cycling gear!

Blue Bell Inn, Great North Road **Wentbridge**
Meals mainly traditional with some continental, £3-£11
Beers: Taylors Landlord, Tetleys, Theakstons

Banks   Barclays, 5 Market Place **Pontefract** (£)
              Natwest, 3 Ropergate **Pontefract** (£)
              Barclays, Bank Street **Hemsworth** (£)

LIVING HISTORY AT PONTEFRACT CASTLE

Today the remnants of this once royal castle at the centre of English history have been carefully lawned and only the bare outline of many of the major features of the main buildings remain. Despite this the amount of space occupied by the ruins still gives you a feeling of the military power and baronial importance the old walls once held within their bounds. There are also good views over much of Pontefract, most noticeably the strange mining landscape of the Prince of Wales colliery.

The castle has been at the very centre of the power struggle in the north whether between rival contestants for the throne of England, or Parliament and King as happened in the Civil War. Originally the home and fortress of the Norman De Lacy nobility it passed through marriage to the Lancaster family, a move that destined the castle to be centre-stage in the forthcoming historical turmoil.

Throughout the coming centuries the castle walls were privy to the imprisonment and murder of Richard II by Henry of Lancaster who usurped the throne as Henry IV. During the 17th century it was a Royalist stronghold that changed hands three times before being demolished, like its western neighbour at Sandal near Wakefield, to prevent action by those still loyal to the son of the executed King Charles I, eventually restored to the throne as Charles II.

After demolition it was used for a variety of unusual purposes including debtors' prison, liquorice cultivation and Victorian park, before eventually being fully excavated under the guidance of the local council, although it is still strictly the Queen's property in right of the Duchy of Lancaster.

Opening times:
Mon-Fri 8.30-dusk/7pm
Sun 2.30-5

35 miles/56km   **Grade 2 (3 after Holmbridge)**

RAIL ACCESS Fitzwilliam, Moorthorpe or South Elmsall/Marsden
(possible 'break' station after 17 miles: Denby Dale)

ROUTE DESCRIPTION

*Pick up the A628 coming out of Hemsworth. Just as you exit the built up area take the first **R**, just past the Bisset Cottage Hotel (s/p South Hiendley and Havercroft) called Robin Lane. First pass the Almshouses, a low brick building now used as a hospital. Come downhill to a T-junction, and **R** towards the town centre. Go past a war memorial on the left then the church on the right. After a small hill turn **L** onto Kirkgate Lane, just past the post office. Ignore next right for Havercroft, and Felkirk church comes into view with the unusual concrete P-shaped structure of a pithead just in front of the town of Royston to your left.*

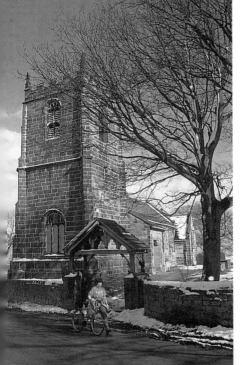

At High Hoyland

Go **R** in front of the church, then **R** at the next junction and straight across the junction with B6428 in half a mile. Ignore the next right for Havercroft and take the next **L** for Notton colliery. Go through the hamlet of Old Royston by passing over Barnsley Canal and a railway bridge respectively. Go over the junction with the B6132, past the Oliver Twist pub on the left. Follow the main road through Notton and just after passing the farms at the far end of the village, **L** down a minor road (Keeper Lane).

Follow through farmland to the A61 and **L** then **R** after 100 yards and start to climb towards Woolley Edge. Coming to the brow of the hill turn **R** and along the edge of this hill for about a mile. Go **R** then **L** at the next two T-junctions respectively, which will bring you into the centre of Woolley village. On coming to the village green turn immediate **L** and follow the road round past a cul-de-sac and **R** down Middle Field Lane. At the end of this lane go **R** at the T-junction for West Bretton. There are good views looking back towards Woolley and further on this road to your left as the M1 comes into view. Go across the first crossroads and in front of the M1 is Savin Royd Wood. Past the small laybys go **L** taking you over the motorway and **L** at the next T-junction into West Bretton.

After the post office take a fork **L** which brings you to the A637. Go **L** then in a few yards **R** by the war memorial. This road leads straight to Bretton Hall College and Yorkshire Sculpture Park. Just before the college gates there is a bridleway on the right, leading you past a small cottage on your right and downhill through an old iron gate and across Bretton lake. NOTE: THE BRIDLEWAY SURFACE IS AN UNSURFACED FARM TRACK - NOT FOR HIGHLY PRIZED TOURING CYCLES.

45

Continue up the track to the main road at High Hoyland Lodge and go **L**. Continue on this road past High Hoyland church (now an activity centre) and **R** at the next T-junction in the village. At the fork just past the Cherry Tree Inn continue right, on the road (the left turn takes you to Cannon Hall in about 1½ miles). After a small rise take the first **L** down Hollin House Lane. Go past a right called Wheatly Hill Lane and then past Deffer Wood on your left. At the end of this long road come to the crossroads with the A635 by the Dunkirk Inn. (Turn **R** onto the A635 the **R** again onto the A636 to bring you to Denby Dale station if exiting here, or straight on at the crossroads if continuing on to Marsden).

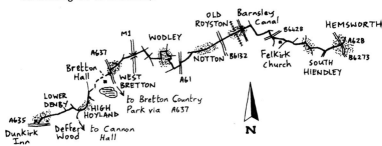

At the Dunkirk Inn go straight over the crossroads with the A635. Carry on under railway bridge and through Upper Denby, going **R** off the main road just after the church. Follow road to T-junction and **R** onto A 629 and shortly **L** onto Windmill Lane. Straight over next crossroads and **L** at the next crossroads. Stay on this road passing over A616 (landmarks: view over Hepworth to your right which lies beneath a 'headland' and on a clear day towards Castle Hill near Almondbury) and over B6106. The route goes straight on this road taking you behind a large and distinctive coniferous plantation after going straight over another crossroads by a phone box at Flaight Hill.

Unmarked roads to the right will take you down to Holmfirth (possible detour). This road loops round the top of the plantation and the Holme Valley settlements of Holmbridge and Upperthong come into view. Ignore left fork for Woodhouse Lane (unsuitable for heavy vehicles). Bear **L** at next fork then ignore all right turns as the road arcs 180 degrees left and you find yourself facing the radio mast on Holme Moss. Go **R** at the next T-junction and **L** just past the junior and infants school.

Bear **R** at every junction before coming to the church. Go **R** onto main road then immediate **L** behind Bridge Tavern. Climb steeply out of Holmbridge. Bear **L** down Bank Top Lane off the more main road. Over the next crossroads just before Digley Reservoir and after another short climb over the next crossroads. Straight over the A635. Descending, watch out for the **L** on the B6107 for Meltham. Shortly go **L** at T-junction with Coach Road.

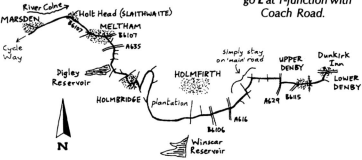

Stay on this B6107 road which climbs out of Meltham and bears left through Holt Head at the White House pub. Follow the side of Colne Valley then descend into Marsden. The Cycle Way is waymarked **L** at the first main junction.

Cannon Hall

• **Hemsworth to Dunkirk Inn** If the mining villages of South Yorkshire don't perhaps strike you as picturesque you can discover hidden gems such as Felkirk church between villages that have suffered more than most from the ravages of modern economic logic and government policies. The area is rich in industrial history, much of its architecture is being reclaimed by nature or has been converted, often for leisure purposes. There are fine views approaching and leaving the village of Woolley. You have just climbed the start of the foothills to the Pennines as you look back going towards Woolley over the flat plain that stretches to the east coast. After the junction at Middle End Lane on the other side of Woolley you eventually see Savin Royd Wood and the M1 behind it.

Although the ancient buildings of Hemsworth and South Hiendley were all but destroyed by the fast track development that accompanied the miraculous rise of the mines, some interesting anomalies remain. The church in Hemsworth, though largely rebuilt, has parts of a 14th century chancel and chapel; and coming into South Hiendley look out for the old brick almshouses on the left, now used as a hospital. Hemsworth markets are Tuesday, Friday, Saturday.

• **Felkirk** St. Peter's church has an unusual war memorial entrance gate and interesting fearsome looking gargoyles on the main tower, which stands in front of an impressively large graveyard.

• **Woolley** The settlements name tells it was a 'wolf haunted glade'. This small stone village retains ancient charm with its church's Norman tympanum and mediaeval round stone over the main door.

• **Woolley Edge** Picturesque and locally popular part of the Wakefield/ Barnsley area. Savin Royd Wood on your left as you go along Woolley Edge reflects the name of a former owner, whilst 'royd' shows it to be a mediaeval wood. Emley Moor TV mast also comes into view on your left; at 1084 feet it is taller than the Eiffel Tower, and is the tallest unsupported structure in the UK.

• **West Bretton and Bretton Hall** Onetime property of the Wentworth family, previously one of the most powerful families in West Yorkshire, Bretton Hall is now a college of education. The family owned estate in Woolley as well and part of their fortune came from silver mining. West Bretton has been well isolated from the total redevelopment of mining areas by the village's links with the above family who controlled much of the village property. Look out for the beautifully shaped war memorial as you turn right towards Bretton Hall, opened before a village throng in 1921 and made from stone found in a defunct menagerie in the house's grounds.

Bretton Hall

This area includes an 18th century landscaped park as well as the **Yorkshire Sculpture Park** within the grounds of Bretton Hall College. A variety of sculptures placed outside in the park create an unusual and distinctive attraction. As well as touring artists there are permanent exhibitions by such greats as Elizabeth Frink and Henry Moore. The Bothy is a distinctive enclosed lawn with good views towards Emley. Sculpture park: free admission. Opening: Spring and Summer, Grounds 10-6, Cafe, gallery, shop 11-4. 01924 375555 for details.

The lower lake, on your left as you cross the bridge is designated a nature reserve open only to members of the Yorkshire Wildfowl Trust. At **Bretton Hall Country Park** have a chat with the deer who are raised in this eighteenth century landscaped garden.You have now started your climb into the foothills of the Pennines towards Holmfirth. There are great views along the rest of this stretch. From the back of the High Hoyland graveyard look out for the large opencast mine workings of Woolley to the left of Barnsley, and several power stations are evident. Spreading round to the right the moors at the edge of the Pennines are apparent. Emley Moor TV mast is a frequent landmark on your right for much of the way. Before the drop down to the Dunkirk Inn it is possible to see Castle Hill at Almondbury on a clear day.

• **Dunkirk Inn to Marsden** This section offers a gradual climb over moorland rewarded by spectacular views as you reach the western edge of the Pennines above Holmfirth and Marsden. The wind turbines after Upper Denby are a surreal and controversial feature of the landscape. Man's influence is also heavily apparent as you view the commercial plantation and numerous reservoirs around Holmfirth. There have been some attempts to redress the balance in nature's favour with the introduction of mountain hares above Digley Reservoir (they are white if you see them in winter).

• **Marsden** still contains strong resonances of its mill town history in the form of the narrow boat canal that runs through it and links to the 3 mile Standedge tunnel to the west. When in use men would have to push boats through this tunnel with their legs due to its extreme narrowness. The canal itself ran from Huddersfield to Manchester and took goods under the Pennines when previously they had been taken over by packhorse. It is the longest and highest altitude tunnel in the country. The Marsden Shuttle (a narrowboat) runs from the railway station to Tunnel End visitor centre (061 339 1332).

LIVING HISTORY

Decaying industry on the Barnsley Canal

It is easy to miss the quiet waters of this neglected epitaph to Yorkshire's industrial heritage as you pass over it at Old Royston. The canal's current sorry state is hardly any indicator of the spectacle it must have presented in its heyday during the early nineteenth century, when it was completed to carry coal dug out of the newly exploited coal seams of the Barnsley field.

On its inauguration the Aire and Calder Navigation Company had two celebratory, fully rigged sloops equipped with cannons sail from its start in Heath near Wakefield to its terminus at the junction with the Dearne and Dove Canal near Barnsley. Eventually however competition from the faster and more efficient road and rail networks meant decay and it was, ironically, the destructive effects of coal mining subsidence that put the final nail in the canal's coffin. Once a major artery in the canal network linking with the Aire and Calder navigation and hence giving access to both coasts it is now slowly being reclaimed by nature. At one point competition between the owners of the canal and another canal company was so intense they engaged in dubious practices such as diverting the course of rivers that fed one anothers' canals.

A LOOK ROUND MARSDEN

1 *Throstle's Nest* Orphans once stayed in this building when brought to Marsden to work in the mills.

2 *Tunnel End* museum and information centre. The former tunnel keeper's cottage traces 2,000 years of transport history. Open April-Oct Tues 2-4, Wed-Fri 10-1 and 2-4, Sat-Sun 10-5; Nov-March Tues 2-4, Wed-Thurs 11-1 and 2-4, Sat-Sun 10.30-4

3 *Tunnel End Inn* Until recently called the Junction Inn, signifying that it was the transfer point for goods from narrowboat to canal before the tunnel was opened. Volunteers are working to reopen the tunnel.

4 *Mellor's Bridge* - old packhorse bridge

5 *Mechanics institute* Built with money raised from Marsden workers for the education and enjoyment of local villagers.

6 *Crowther, Bruce and Company* A private mill still fully working!

7 *Lakeside bridge* Wool is still unloaded here for processing in the mill.

8 Look out for the *tenterstones* here which were once used in the textile industry for stretching and drying cloth.

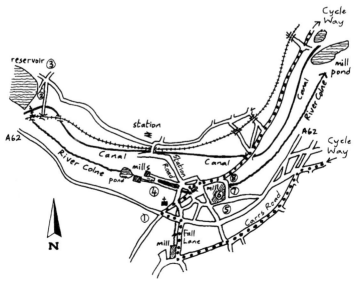

CIRCULAR ROUTE

SANDAL CASTLE AND WOOLLEY EDGE

23 miles/37km   Very easy Grade 2

*From Sandal station turn **L** onto Agbrigg Road and shortly hit the A61 Barnsley road. Dismount and cross the road going **R** after the no entry sign onto the road with the wall at the end of it. At the top of this road (Sandal Avenue) **R** to a T-junction and go **L**. This brings you to Sandal Castle on your right. Continue on this road, after a stroll around the castle if you wish, again meeting the A61 and crossing almost straight over (**R** then immediate **L**) down Chevet Lane by the Three Horses pub. Quite shortly take a **L** s/p for the golf club and Walton Hall (Walton Station Lane) going down a short country road to a T-junction. Go **R** here then **L** down Shay Lane over a railway bridge on the B6378. Look out for the s/p to Walton Hall and the golf club (the Balk) and go **R** down here if you want to see Walton Hall - see 'along the way'. If not, keep straight on, on the circular route.*

*Pass through the suburb of Walton and continue under two railway bridges and **R** at the next T-junction after you've come into Crofton. Stay on this road through town first going past the church on your left and as the road bends right, past the Slipper pub. This road takes you past the anglers' country park on the right and through the village of Wintersett, continuing on this road. The road then goes over Wintersett Reservoir to a T-junction where you go **R**. Proceed through the quaint village of Cold Hiendley to another T-junction and **L**. The next **R** for Notton and Woolley takes you over the old Barnsley Canal and over a railway bridge past a small row of cottages. At the next crossroads go straight over.*

*Go through Notton and **L** down Keeper Lane on the edge of the village just after farm buildings. On meeting the A61 go **L** then immediate **R**. Go uphill until you come over a rise and then **R**. Follow this road*

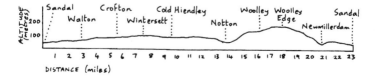

along a natural ridge, then **R** then **L** at the next two T-junctions to Woolley village centre. Go **L** by the green, down the High Street past a dead end and the church. After Middle Field Lane on the right go **R** down Gypsy Lane. At the T-junction go **R** and then at the second set of crossroads go **R,** just past the lay-by. Straight over the next set of crossroads then **R** at the next set (s/p Woolley Hall college 1) bringing you full circle round the Woolley plateau and **L** down the next minor road, Parson Lane. At the next two T-junctions go **R** and **L** respectively onto the A61.

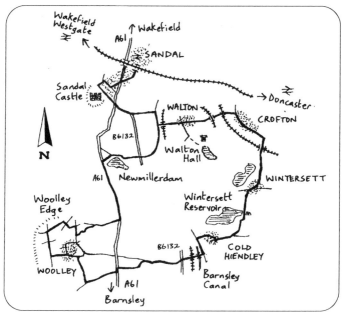

This major road leads downhill to the large lake on your right called Newmillerdam. Just past the lake go **R** into the pub car park and look for the small no access road just past the lake entrance gates. Go up this small, steep lane and **R** onto Hill Top Lane. Follow this road for just over a mile over the B6132 and back into Walton. Take the **L** which retraces your earlier steps, just after Shay Lane on your right. **R** at the next T-junction brings you onto Chevet Lane and **R** at the end back onto the A61. Follow this main road for a short while and a little after seeing Sandal Magma church on the right look for Agbrigg Road on the **R** which leads you back to the station.

• **Sandal Castle** Dating back to the Norman conquest of the north of England, these crumbling ruins sit in a commanding position on high ground and were once the site of buildings that were a testament to the power of factions competing for the throne of England. The plan below shows the main features of the main castle buildings as they would have been after its enlargement in the thirteenth century. After military conquest by Norman nobles it became a royal tax gathering and administration centre.

Richard of York was killed here by Lancastrians at the battle of Wakefield in 1463 and Richard III subsequently rebuilt the castle into a major northern stronghold. The building was all but destroyed by the military bombardment during the siege by Roundheads and was one of the last Royalist strongholds to survive. It remained in decrepit state and was partially covered with earth by victorious Parliamentarians to prevent its reuse by Royalists. Today's remains were finally uncovered and restored during the 1960's.

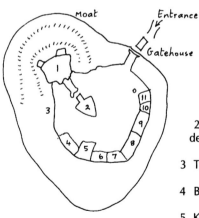

SANDAL CASTLE

as it would have been in the 13th century

1 The Keep - last stronghold in case of siege

2 The Barbican - last line of defence before the keep

3 Thick defensive 'curtain wall'

4 Bakehouse and Brewhouse

5 Kitchen   6 Larder

7 Lodging Chamber   8 Great Hall   9 Great Chamber

10 Privy Chamber   11 Constable's Lodging

• **Walton Hall** A short detour down the Balk in Walton, this hotel is the former home of the eccentric naturalist Charles Waterton, whose strange taxidermy experiments can be seen at Wakefield Museum on Wood Street. After visits to various corners of the world he experimented in joining various parts of dead animals together to create fabulous new creatures; it would be interesting to see what reaction such activity would get if carried out in today's more 'animal conscious' climate!

• **Woolley** The village is set impressively on a raised ledge giving great views, and the route purposely twists around 360-degrees of this beautiful topographical feature. Strict planning laws have preserved much of the village's charm and many of its old buildings.

LIVING HISTORY IN THE YORKSHIRE COALFIELD
Coal not dole

Passing near Royston Pit and through Woolley it is hard to imagine that this area, as part of the generally militant Yorkshire coalfield, was at the centre of the 1984-5 national miner's strike. Only the young and those with short memories will forget the drama and confrontation of the largest ever strike in the UK to have lasted for more than a year.

Shortly after the second world war the coal industry employed almost three quarters of a million people. Automation and overcapacity had reduced this by a staggering 75% before the strike in 1984. A dogmatically right wing government with a secret agenda of privatisation and a large programme of pit closures met with a hard core of resistant miners lead by a flamboyant leader. Ironically Arthur Scargill was not opposed to a slimming down of the coal system but wanted this on the union's terms, not the government's.

At the beginning of the strike Woolley colliery was the first pit in the country listed to receive a new computerised operating system for the whole mine, but closed after the strike. Villages whose economy revolved around mining such as South Hiendley and Hemsworth never really recovered from the divisiveness of the strike, when the mining community was bitterly split over whether to strike in the absence of a national ballot. They found themselves unluckily trapped between a government committed to nuclear power at the cost of running down the coal industry and selling it off, and a union which employed questionable tactics and whose tendency to split under pressure caused much internecine strife.

CIRCULAR ROUTE

ABOVE AND AROUND DENBY DALE;
INGBIRCHWORTH AND CANNON HALL

18 miles/29km   Grade 2

This route proves it is ι   necessary to travel deep into the Pennines
for truly beautiful scer   y. Denby Dale, the starting point, is an ideal
base fr   which to explore the surrounding countryside. A climb up
to sr ιacular views over the reservoirs around Ingbirchworth is
fo" ved by a visit to Thurlstone and an equally spectacular descent
ᶠ ᴵally taking in the splendour of the stately home converted to
museum, Cannon Hall. I did this route on a mountain bike one mid-
winter when the roads where not cleared by snow ploughs. The deep
snow had forced a fox to come out of Deffer Woods and look for food
in the nearby farm settlements. The route is definitely a hard grade 2;
it mixes ascents and descents together. Although the main climb is to
a high point above Ingbirchworth there are numerous other drops and
ascents, however even taken steadily it is easy to get round in a day,
or even half a day for fit and experienced cyclists. Do pace yourself
though as the climbs continue right towards the end of the route.

*From the railway station in Denby Dale at the base of the huge
viaduct, come down the track to the main road and **L** onto the main
road into the heart of the village. Take the second **R** on to Miller Hill
and climb for about two-thirds of a mile to the main road. Go **L** then
immediate **R** opposite the Dunkirk Inn (s/p New Mill and Holmfirth).
Uphill continue through Upper Denby and first **R** past the church. At
the A629 **R** into the small settlement of High Flatts and first **L** down
Windmill Lane. Gently climb and descend to crossroads and **L** here.
At the first staggered junction bear **L** which will bring you to the edge
of Ingbirchworth Reservoir. At the start of the reservoir look for the*

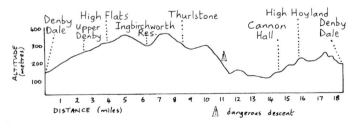

first **R** up a minor road which brings you to the top of Spicer Hill where an impressive array of wind turbines are located. **L** at the T-junction by the turbines and continue to a crossroads and **L** into the village of Thurlstone. You will come to the centre of Thurlstone on High Royd Lane which brings you to a T-junction; go **L** here and follow the road round looking for the small street of Matthew Gap.

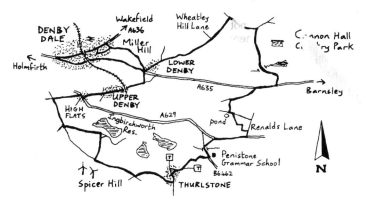

Go to the end and **R**, then at the next junction bear **L** avoiding the road leading straight on marked as a dead end (this is tricky navigation - refer to OS map if you go astray here). Exit at the B6462 by Penistone Grammar School and go left. After a bridge over a small stream look for a minor **R** leading to the A629, going **R** again and two-thirds of a mile down this main road to a minor **L** (Renalds Lane). Then immediate **L** past a no access sign (for motorbikes and cars). The steep descent leads to a T-junction; **L** then **R** again immediately after the pond on your left. Bear **R** at every opportunity until you meet the A635 (s/p Gunthwaite in the direction you have come from). **R** on the main road for about a mile until a **L** (s/p Cannon Hall).

This leads over a small hump back bridge past Cannon Hall country park and museum, which makes an ideal break before the final 5 miles (there is a cafe in the garden centre on your left). Enter High Hoyland after continuing from Cannon Hall and at T-junction in the village go **L** and uphill. Take the next left and follow this minor road for 2½ miles until the junction with A635 at the Dunkirk Inn. Go **R** onto the main road and **R** immediately. You now retrace your steps into Denby Dale as this road brings you to the bottom of Miller Hill and **L** leads back to the station.

• **Denby Dale** Most famous for its pie hall, home of the 'largest pie in the world'. Actually the most striking feature of the village from the distance is the massive viaduct carrying the train line from Wakefield to Penistone and Barnsley.

• A general feature of the landscape is its more 'natural' appearance as the land rises from the intensely cultivated fields of the east into the Pennines; here more woodland has been preserved. Note the rolling nature of the Pennine foothills both from above Ingbirchworth Reservoir and again particularly on the descent to the A635, before Cannon Hall park.

• **Cannon Hall Country Park** This commanding country residence was built by the Spencer family in the late 17th century. The two wings to the house were later additions. The Spencer family were one of a syndicate to control the profits from the charcoal and iron industries in Derbyshire and the West Riding. There are acres of rolling greenery to stroll around, and beautiful formal gardens round the house, which is set impressively above some small falls where the river Dearne rises. Open Tues-Sat 10.30-5.00, Sunday 12.00-7.00. Tearooms, WC and model farm. Admission to grounds and house free.

The windfarm above Ingbirchworth

SERVICES

Accommodation

The Old Manor House, 19 Sycamore Lane **West Bretton**   01924 830324
£15 (evening meal sometimes available at £7)   Facilities: S;D;L

The Poppies, 8 Cobbler Hall **West Bretton**   01924 830317
£15   Facilities: S;D;L

High Hoyland Activity Centre **High Hoyland**
Unusual converted church sleeps up to 24 people
£20 per night basic charge plus £2 per person. Cheap if there's a large group.
Contact Rachael Davies 01924 830261
Self catering with WC, showers, gas and electricity meters

Forest Farm Bunkhouse and Guesthouse, Mount Road **Marsden**
Contact Huddersfield Tourist Information for further details
Bunkhouse: £7.50, self catering
Guesthouse: £14 (evening meal £7)
Discounts for children   Facilities: S;D

Coach and Horses Hotel, Manchester Road **Marsden**
(on A62 three miles west) 01484 844241
£25 (doubles only, used as singles) £40 Double
Breakfast £3.75   Facilities: S;D;L

Food
Cherry Tree Inn **High Hoyland**
Meals generally under £5   Beers: John Smiths, Ruddles, Courage Directors

Dunkirk Inn **Lower Denby**
Bar meals under £5   Beers: Tetleys, Marston's Pedigree, Theakstons

The route takes you past a fish and chip shop in South Hiendley

Bothy Cafe, Yorkshire Sculpture Park **West Bretton** Continental/English
snacks and wine up to £5 Open 11-4

Travellers Rest, Slaithwaite Road **Meltham** (on route exiting Meltham)
Meals generally under £6   Beers: Burtonwood

White Horse **Slaithwaite** (on the route on B6107 before descent to Marsden)
Meals up to about £8   Beers: Taylors, Tetleys

Bridge Tavern **Marsden**
Meals generally under £5   Beers: Courage, Ruddles

Railway Inn, Station Road **Marsden** (by railway station)
Meals under £5   Beers: Burtonwood

Rose and Crown **Marsden** (on the route climbing out of Marsden)
Meals £4-£5   Beers: Tetleys, guest beer

STAGE SIX

MARSDEN TO HAWORTH

36 miles/58km   **Grade 3**

RAIL ACCESS Marsden/Haworth (Keighley & Worth Valley Railway
(possible 'break' station after 22 miles: Mytholmroyd)

ROUTE DESCRIPTION

*Approaching Marsden on the B6107 from Stage 5 split off **L** coming
into the town down Carrs Road, and continue on this road going **R** at
the roundabout. At the end of this road jink **L** onto A62 then
immediate **R** past Marsden church. At next T-junction go **R** onto road
in town centre then **L** off main road at the Swan pub. Follow this minor
road until you come to the end of it at a T-junction. Right is marked
a dead end so go **L** and under a railway bridge. GO IMMEDIATE LEFT
UNDER THE RAILWAY BRIDGE MARKED UNSUITABLE FOR VEHI-
CLES OVER 6' WIDE. THE CYCLE WAY IS WAYMARKED RIGHT AT
THIS JUNCTION - THIS IS INCORRECT.*

Hebden Bridge

There is then a very steep climb in a long right handed curve going past very minor turnings on the left and right. A radio mast should come into view intermittently on your left and after a short while pass the Rose and Crown pub and come to a crossroads going *L* onto Cop Hill Side (straight on is a dead end). The road loops round the top of Scout Wood nestling in a small valley to your right, and the road joins Tyas Lane coming in obliquely from the right as you continue onto Laund Road.

At the next junction Intake Lane joins from the right. Carry straight on here past Burnt Platts Lane on the left. At the next T-junction with Pole Gate go *L* and *L* at the next turning, bringing you to the A640 where you go *L* again. You then have two options.

1. For the scenic route, including steep down and uphill sections, take next *R* which brings you down Sledge Gate bending left past a right turn to reservoir car park. Round the head of the reservoir (ignoring the right for the activity club) climb to the main B6114 then *R*.

2. Continue on A640 for 1½ miles then go right onto B6114.

The B6114 crosses over the M62 then acute first *L* at Ringstone Edge Reservoir. Stay on the more major tarmac road ignoring any minor turnings, bringing you right next to the overspill of Booth Wood Reservoir, bend round 180 degrees and go *L* at the T-junction with the A672. In about a third of a mile go *R* off the main road just before the Turnpike Inn up Pike End Road. Follow this quiet country road over Rishworth Moor (don't go into Rishworth itself), going *L* at the only T-

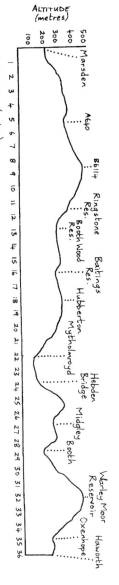

61

junction you meet and over Baitings Reservoir. **L** onto the A58 then immediate **R** down Blue Ball Road (s/p Blue Ball Inn). This is a climb from the head of the Ryburn Valley over the Pennine hills to the Calder Valley. Fork **L** after Blue Ball Inn then **L** just after this. Go **L** at every opportunity for the next 6 miles until the Shepherds Rest pub in Hubberton village. Go **L** at the turning next to the pub and bear **L** ignoring next right turn.

Now going down Mirey Lane go straight over the next crossroads and **R** when faced with 'no through' sign on road in front of you. Descend down Hathershelf Lane then **L** at T-junction onto Scout Road, then 1½ miles to a T-junction in Mytholmroyd, going **R**. On over the bridge in Mytholmroyd, **L** on A646 and 1½ miles into Hebden Bridge centre. Go **R** at the traffic lights in front of the Tourist Information Centre, on to Bridge Gate.

Through town centre to T-junction with A6033 (Keighley Road). **R** onto the main road then immediate **L** (s/p Birchcliffe Centre) climbing steeply past Stubbings school on the right. Go past the Birchcliffe Centre on your left and turn **L** down minor road (Sandygate) s/p link path to Calderdale Way. Take the first fork **R** then **L** in front of the bungalow in 100 yards (right is a rough track). At the T-junction by the Hare and Hounds pub go **R**, (left takes you to Chiserley in a third of a mile where there is the Automobilia Car Museum). Continue on this good wide road into Midgley, through village centre, forking **L** by the defunct Sportsman's Inn at end of village. Continue for about 1½ miles skirting Midgley Moor until you face a dead end (High House Lane) where you fork **R**. The road hairpins right, ignoring straight on (hairpin waymarked).

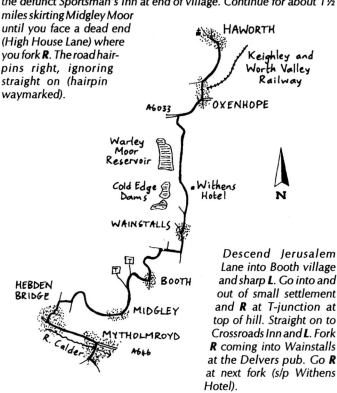

Descend Jerusalem Lane into Booth village and sharp **L**. Go into and out of small settlement and **R** at T-junction at top of hill. Straight on to Crossroads Inn and **L**. Fork **R** coming into Wainstalls at the Delvers pub. Go **R** at next fork (s/p Withens Hotel).

Continue over the moor past this hotel, by unsurfaced road next to Warley Moor Reservoir. Continue over moor for about 4 miles until T-junction with A6033 going **R** into Oxenhope. Go **L** at next crossroads and past Oxenhope station (with steam train museum at head of Keighley and Worth Valley Railway). **R** at next T-junction and into Haworth (about 1 mile). At first T-junction **L** then immediate **L** up cobbled main street bringing you to the start/finish point of the whole Cycle Way.

• **Hebden Bridge** Remaining Celtic in origin and untouched by the Romans, the town as you see it today is largely the product of the textile industry whose mills and solid stone architecture have come to dominate it. With increasing demand and the march of progress, hand loom weaving was replaced with water power and eventually mechanical power. More than any other town on the route Hebden Bridge is an ideal chance to see an abundance of fascinating industrial relics. Everywhere you turn there seems to be a monument to the industry, perseverance and adaptability that allowed the early industrial revolution to flourish in such a small space, crammed, as it is, in the small valley space between four protruding fingers of the southern Pennines. Market day is Thursday.

Originally mills were powered by water wheels as steep valley sides here were the natural topography to provide such natural water power. As mills became increasingly powered by steam the industry was pulled towards the lower Calder Valley, and major reservoirs above the valley were constructed to provide 'soft' water for bigger mill towns further down the valley, Hebden Bridge experienced local competition. This combined with foreign competition and lack of investment to send the industry into a declining spiral. Population reached its lowest in the mid twentieth century but visit today and you will see plenty of evidence of the resurgence of a bustling market town amidst the ruined relics of an age never to return. See page 66 for a look round Hebden Bridge.

• **Hardcastle Crags**, 400 acres of National Trust property are easily accessed from the Tourist Information Centre. There is also an interesting riverside walk signposted which begins at the TIC. Along this walk and at Gibson Mill in Hardcastle Crags is a fine old example of an abandoned cotton mill, originally water power as evidenced by the dam next to it and later converted to steam. Because of the exceptional flowered woodland, reminiscent of wooded alpine scenes, this area was once known as 'Little Switzerland'. The area can be reached on foot from the circular Heptonstall route from the Slack area.

• **Midgley**, the small incongruous village after Hebden Bridge is fairly typical of many of the smaller towns above the main valley in this area. Once thriving with a number of pubs and shops this village is now a shadow of its former self. Originally cleared by Saxons as agricultural settlements above the marshy valleys, such settlements later came to rely heavily on the local 'hybrid' residents turning their hands to farming the hostile land and hand weaving, at first a cottage based family centred industry. Of course they found themselves completely uncompetitive with the wholesale mechanisation of the textile industry. Nowadays such places are a mix of farming and commuting activities.

Left: Scammonden Reservoir   *Methodist chapel, Heptonstall*

A LOOK ROUND HEBDEN BRIDGE

1 *Fustian cutting workshop* Identify this building on your right as you enter on the main road by two rows of numerous mullioned windows. These provided sufficient light for the hand work of cutting loops in a weave of cloth to produce a corduroy effect ('cutting fustian').

2 *Princess bridge* over the Rochdale Canal. This bridge was widened by the Lancashire and Yorkshire Railway company at the end of the nineteenth century. From Station Road over the bridge there is a particularly good view down the canal which used to connect the easterly Calder and Hebble navigation to the Bridgewater and Ashton narrow canals. The Rochdale Canal Society has restored much of the length of the canal. There are plans to 'unblock' a final section and link it to the national network shortly.

3 *Hope baptist church* Built in classical style in 1857, it provided services for Hebden Bridge's population of this breakaway religion.

4 *National Westminster Bank* The window surrounds and roof gables are typical of earlier local architecture. The picturesque quality of the facade has meant the bank has featured in a national TV commercial.

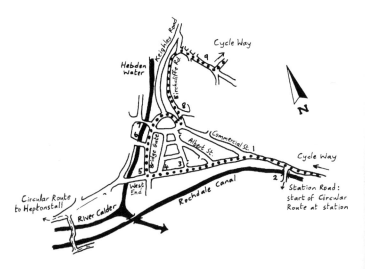

5 *Tourist Information Centre*

6 *The old bridge* A bridge is recorded here as early as 1508 and formed part of the nucleus of early Hebden Bridge, along with a corn mill and other smaller buildings. Various inscriptions on the bridge range from 1602 to 1890. The Hole in the Wall pub near the bridge sits on the site of many earlier inns, which exploited the growth of regular traffic over Hebden Water because of the existence of a reliable stone bridge; a relatively rare phenomenon in those days.

7 *St. George's Bridge* This unusual cast iron bridge was opened in 1893 and opened up a whole new area of building for the town, hence most of the buildings around the market area date from shortly after this time.

8 *Stubbings school* The first school to be built in Hebden Bridge. The 1870 education act actually legalised the spending of local authority funds on universal education.

9 *The Birchcliffe Centre* This building is in fact a superb mock renaissance style baptist chapel, built in 1899. It was closed in 1974 due to dwindling attendances and is now primarily a conference centre (extensively converted on the interior by a social trust, for this purpose).

Above Hebden Bridge

HEPTONSTALL AND AROUND COLDEN CLOUGH

7½ miles/12km   Grade 3

This is a relatively short day ride but it is one of my favourites, taking in some of the most breathtaking scenery in West Yorkshire; the sombre rolling moors above Hebden Bridge, the ancient village of Heptonstall and if you have a bike capable of off road conditions then a beautiful bridleway alternative route, through the craggy Colden Clough which includes dramatic mill ruins. It starts with a very long stiff climb for which low gearing and good stamina are essential but this extended effort is rewarded as you come onto the 'tops' for the majority of the journey, with consistently splendid panoramas. The descent is similarly steep and dramatic.

*Start in front of Hebden Bridge station and go **R** down the small tarmac path and through the concrete bollards at the end. **R** takes you under a railway bridge and round the corner onto Palace House Road. Climb over this small hill staying on this road and dropping downhill through two sets of traffic lights, crossing the bridges over the canal and river respectively. **L** onto the main A646 and uphill until the sign for Heptonstall (a hairpin back **R**). There is no right turn allowed here so dismount and cross onto this road, proceeding up this very steep climb and forking first **L** (s/p Heptonstall) and eventually onto the cobbled main street of Heptonstall village after 1¼ miles of very hard work!*

*The route continues on this cobbled street through Heptonstall and to a T-junction going **L** into the small village of Slack. On this road look out for Stoodley Pike monument to the left, which crowns higher moorland to the south. Through Slack and carry straight on in front*

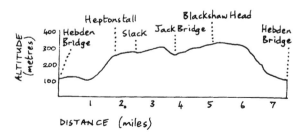

of the Zion church, (s/p Blackshaw Head). Follow this road through the terraces of Colden and drop and bend left to Jack Bridge (SEE ALTERNATIVE ROUTE). Continue on this road into Blackshaw Head.

Take the first left just before the Shoulder of Mutton pub. Now on Badger Lane you cross both the Calderdale Way and Pennine Way walking routes. After a great view of Heptonstall with Eaves Wood dropping away in front of it the road hairpins sharply descending into the settled valley bottom. On joining the main road go **L** and then through the town centre looking for a turning onto Station Road, which takes you over the canal and back to the station.

ALTERNATIVE FOR BIKES CAPABLE OF OFF ROAD CYCLING: Coming out of Jack Bridge on an uphill right hand bend there is an unsignposted bridleway to the left which takes a spectacular cut back towards Heptonstall via a mini-gorge and old mill ruins. Continue on this track which passes a couple of houses and disused dams on the left entering beautiful woods which cling to the side of the clough. **Warning**: there is a steep drop to the left and the track is unsurfaced and quite bumpy in places; keep under control at all times and away from the edge. After entering the woods take the first **L** which hairpins back on your entry route. This crosses the river via a couple of houses and Lumb Mill ruins. The track then hairpins up the opposite side of the valley and is steep and muddy - true mountain bike terrain.

Rejoin a tarmac road alongside a house contained by long stone wall on your right (on the ascent stick to the main path and ignore all minor trails). Hit the road you exited Heptonstall on and turn **L**. On coming to the T-junction in Slack this time go **R**. This road then enters woods above Hebden Water and descends back into Hebden Bridge giving you good views over Nutclough. It rejoins your ascent, so on joining the A646 dismount and walk across this road and **L** on the main road back into the town centre. To return to the rail station go through the town centre and look for a bridge over the canal (good views down the canal) which is Station Road.

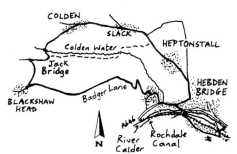

• Starting and finishing the route by the train station is an ideal opportunity to explore the local stretch of the Rochdale Canal.

• **Heptonstall** is an ancient village packed with history. Its name betrays a Saxon origin but the town's heyday was based on the advent of a local hand loom weaving industry. At its peak the village's inhabitants numbered over 4,000 compared to today's 2,000. The industry was effectively finished with the advent of water powered mills in the valley bottom. A Royalist garrison was based here during the war but vacated the town before a Royalist force from the main base of Halifax managed to wade across the river and storm Heptonstall. It is also famous for 'coining' activity during the 18th century. The coin counterfeiters were quite ruthless criminals who filed the edges off coins and made the filings into new coins, whilst 're-rimming' the old coins.

• Looking left on the road going from Heptonstall to Slack the **Stoodley Pike** monument stands isolated and commanding on higher moorland above the Calder Valley. Originally built by local subscription to celebrate victory over Napoleon in 1814, the present monument was completed in 1856 after being struck by lightning. A third of the way up its 120 ft height is a public viewing gallery. Its purpose is radically different to the many traditional post world war one and two monuments which usually mourn the loss of the dead or the 'glory' of victory; an inscription on it makes clear it celebrates the outbreak of peace.

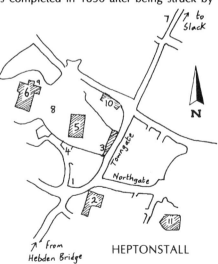

HEPTONSTALL

A LOOK ROUND HEPTONSTALL

1 *Guide map of town*

2 *Stag Cottage* - one of the oldest surviving cottages in Heptonstall

3 *Cloth Hall* - here hand woven cloth was once sold to local traders

4 *Old Grammar School* - founded in 1642 from a legacy from a local rector and lord of the manor. It is now a museum and contains a reconstruction of the original grammar school.

5 *Old Church* - evoking an eerie sense of 'gothic horror' this ruined church was originally built between 1256 and 1260. The 'great storm' of 1847 caused much damage to the tower and the church was subsequently abandoned in favour of its new neighbour.

6 *New Church* of St Thomas the Apostle - replaced the old church. The clock in the tower was a feature of the old church from 1809-1854.

7 *Old hand operated water pump* A throwback to the days before piped water, this was one of four pumps in Heptonstall.

8 *Old Graveyard* said to contain over 100,000 bodies. Some gravestones have been used twice, with one inscription being laid face down. Look for the hanged coiner, David Hartley.

9 The site of the 'pinnacle' from the tower which fell off when struck by lightning

10 *Weaver's Square* - Beautiful cobbled square on site of previous weavers' cottages

11 *Methodist Chapel* - a splendid octagonal building of 1764

SERVICES

Accommodation

Blue Ball Inn **Baitings**   £17.60

1 Primrose Terrace, **Hebden Bridge** 01422 844747
£12.50   Facilities: S;D (bikes can be taken inside if only a couple)

Food

Blue Ball Inn **Baitings**
Meals £2-£9.50   Beers: Taylors, Bass, Theakstons Closed Tues lunchtimes

Shepherds Rest Inn **Hubberton** (on route before descent into Mytholmroyd)
Meals £1.50-£4.50   Beers: Theakstons, Youngers, guest beers
Closed weekday lunchtimes

Hare and Hounds **Chiserley** (on route after Hebden Bridge)
Meals £1.50-£7.50   Beers: Taylors
Closed Summer lunchtimes Mon-Tues, Winter lunchtimes Mon-Thurs

Mount Skip Inn **Wadsworth** (on route after Hebden Bridge)
Meals £1.50-£9.50   Beers: Taylors Landlord, Golden Best, Ram Tam
Closed Monday lunchtimes Oct-April

Crossroads Inn **Wainstalls**
Meals for around £3   Beers: Vaux
Closed Winter weekday lunchtimes except Fridays

Withens Hotel, Cold Edge Road **Wainstalls**
(on route between Wainstalls and Warley Moor)
Meals £1.50-£3.50   Beers: Taylors, John Smiths, Tetleys
Closed Mon-Fri lunchtimes in winter

Camping

Pennine Camp and Caravan Site, High Greenwood House **Heptonstall**
01422 842287   £2 per night   Facilities: S; hot showers

Mount Skip Inn **Wadsworth** Contact Rosemary Earle 01422 842765

Jerusalem Farm Campsite, Jerusalem Lane, Booth **Luddenden** 01422 883246
£2 per night   Facilities: WC, hot water, showers. Groups book in advance.
Closed Nov-March

Bridge Tavern **Marsden** Contact Mrs. Robinson 01484 684162

Crossroads Inn **Wainstalls** advise they will let cyclists camp in the beer
garden. Contact 01422 245316 for details

Group centres
 The Birchcliffe Centre, Hebden Road **Hebden Bridge**   01422 843626
4-bedded en-suite rooms from £9.40 per person. Larger groups only
Full catering available

Slack Top Centre, Mount Zion Baptist Chapel (**Heptonstall** circular route)
Various limitations and surcharges on numbers and concessions. Only
groups with 'Christian Input' can use at weekend. 01422 842874

Banks   Lloyds, 4 Peel Street **Marsden**
              Natwest, 2 Crown Street **Hebden Bridge** (£)
              Lloyds, Albert Street **Hebden Bridge** (£)

Cycle shop
D.C. Mansfield, 9 New Road **Mytholmroyd** 01422 884397

Tourist Information
49-51 Huddersfield Road **Holmfirth** 01484 684992
3-5 Albion Street **Huddersfield** 01484 430808
1 Bridge Gate **Hebden Bridge** 01422 843831

CIRCULAR ROUTE

ABOVE OXENHOPE TO NEWSHOLME DEAN

16 miles/26km   Grade 2 (with one long grade 3 climb)

The best way to get to the start of this route is via the delightful Keighley and Worth Valley Railway, especially if you think you'd enjoy the sensation of travelling on a steam drawn carriage (see overleaf for details). You'll climb north-west out of Haworth to the small settlement of Stanbury and finally over the wild rolling moors around Newsholme Dean (the latter word indicating you'll pass a small picturesque valley). You'll complete the run by coming back towards Oxenhope down the main street in Haworth past all the various Bronte 'sights' where you can stop, if so inclined. Haworth is perhaps best avoided in high summer if you want to steer clear of large crowds of Bronte 'pilgrims'.

This circular route overlaps significantly with Stage 6 of the Cycle Way but I liked the countryside so much I wanted to incorporate it into a smaller route. There are plenty of eating places along the whole of the route, especially at Stanbury which seems to consist of nothing but pubs!

*Starting in Oxenhope station yard turn **R** and come to a T-junction going **L** (the Cycle Way is waymarked right at this junction). This leads you uphill, down a one-way street and past a school on the right. On hitting the main road go **R** and carry on climbing past the Bay Horse pub and at the first telephone box **R** onto Shaw Lane, (s/p Stanbury & Colne). Continue out of Oxenhope on this road (ignoring all cross-roads), past Penistone Hill Country Park on the right, and just after dropping down and going past Lower Laithe Reservoir on your left*

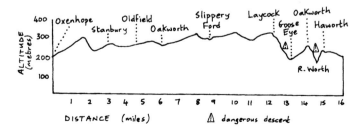

come to T-junction and go **L** (s/p Stanbury & Colne). Coming out of Stanbury you can pick out the broad landscape around Ponden Reservoir, for which you are now heading. Very soon after descending past Ponden Mill look for a hairpin **R** onto Oldfield Lane. Climb through Oldfield and on to a T-junction. Go **R** onto the main road and after going over moorland into Oakworth, onto Commercial Street then immediate **L** just after the Golden Fleece Inn.

At the first T-junction go **L** then take the next split **L** down Wide Lane. You are now following the Cycle Way so at the next T-junction by the cemetery and church go **L**. Your journey now takes you around onto beautiful moors. Go over a small bridge and climb and drop down quite steeply taking the **R** a short while after this steep drop down Coppy Lane, soon turning into Greystones Lane.

Follow the north side of Newsholme Dean then drop down to a more main road going **L** and after a short hard climb first **R** (Tarn Lane). After following the edge of Steeton Moor go **R** down Back Lane, leading you into Laycock village, coming to T-junction with the cemetery on your left and the chapel over the road. Go **R** and just coming out of the village look for a **L** down Goose Eye Brow (s/p Haworth 1½). Descend steeply to go over a bridge leading to the outskirts of Oakworth. Go past a left leading to Keighley and across the next set of crossroads with the cemetery marked on the right.

Past Wide Lane on the right, drop down to the main road and **R** retracing your route in the opposite direction past the Golden Fleece. Now climbing the hill out of Oakworth look for a small left called Tim Lane (marked as 'leading to Haworth') and **L** down it. After a dramatic *drop and climb (a real killer) emerge into the back of Haworth and go across the main road and, dismounting, down the no access road which will take you down the cobbled main street. At the bottom just off the main road take the **R**, Bridgehouse Lane (s/p Oxenhope 2). Coming into Oxenhope look for the **L** down Moorhouse Lane downhill to a **L** for Mill Lane completing your journey at the station.*

ALONG THE WAY

• **Keighley and Worth Valley Railway** is run by volunteers. The line runs from the main BR station in Keighley through several stations, the last two being Haworth and Oxenhope. The majority of services are steam powered. Services are run every weekend throughout the year and daily in the summer season. Bikes are generally allowed on the steam services as long as it does not involve large groups of cyclists. The station at Oxenhope is located next to a small railway museum with free admission. The railway's cinematic potential was realised in the film *The Railway Children*. For general aspects of the service ring 01535 645214 (speaking timetable 01535 647777).

• Superb views around the Worth Valley and Newsholme Dean: going above the Worth Valley through Oldfield, Haworth sits commandingly on the edge of the moors; approaching Newsholme Dean after Oakworth cemetery, views further improve; after you climb onto the road above Laycock there are superb vistas over Keighley and of the moors to the north; from the top of Tim Lane look out towards Haworth and Oxenhope and Haworth moors behind.

ghley & Worth Valley Railway

RECORD OF THE JOURNEY

Date	Place	Miles daily	Miles total	Times arrive	Times depart	Comments
	Haworth	-	-			
	Oakworth	6	6			
	Silsden	16	16			
	Ilkley	21	21			
	Menston	4	25			
	Bramhope	8	29			
	A61	13	34			
	Collingham	19	40			
	Wetherby	23	44			
	Boston Spa	3	47			
	Bramham	6	50			
	Aberford	14	58			
	Ledston	18	62			
	Castleford	21	65			
	Pontefract	5	70			
	Darrington	8	73			
	Wentbridge	11	76			
	Badsworth	14	79			
	Hemsworth	16	81			

STAGE ONE

STAGE TWO

STAGE THREE

STAGE FOUR

Date	Place	Miles		Times		Comments
		daily	total	arrive	depart	
	South Hiendley	3	84			
	Notton	5	86			
	Woolley	9	90			
	West Bretton STAGE FIVE	11	92			
	High Hoyland	14	95			
	Lower Denby	17	98			
	Upper Denby	19	100			
	Holmbridge	29	110			
	Meltham	33	114			
	Marsden	35	116			
	Scammonden/M62	10	126			
	Baitings	16	132			
	Hubberton	18	134			
	Mytholmroyd	22	138			
	Hebden Bridge	24	140			
	Midgley STAGE SIX	27	143			
	Wainstalls	29	145			
	Oxenhope	35	151			
	Haworth	36	152			

THE MOUNTAIN BIKE CODE OF CONDUCT

RIGHTS OF WAY

* *Bridleways* - open to cyclists, but you must give way to walkers and horse riders

* *Byways* - Usually unsurfaced tracks open to cyclists. As well as walkers and cyclists, you may meet occasional vehicles which also have a right of access.

* *Public footpaths* - no right to cycle exists

Look out for posts from the highway, or waymarking arrows (blue for bridleways, red for byways and yellow for footpaths)

NB: The above rights do not apply in Scotland

OTHER ACCESS

* *Open land* - on most upland, moorland and farmland, cyclists normally have no right of access without express permission of the landowner.

* *Towpaths* - a British Waterways cycling permit is required for cyclists wishing to use their canal towpaths.

* *Pavements* - cycling is not permitted on pavements

* *Designated cycle paths* - look out for designated cycle paths or bicycle routes which may be found in urban areas, on Forestry Commission land, disused railway lines or other open spaces.

OTHER INFORMATION

* Cyclists must adhere to the Highway Code. A detailed map is recommended for more adventurous trips.

SAFETY

* Ensure that your bike is safe to ride and prepared for all emergencies
* You are required by law to display working lights after dark (front and rear)
* Always carry some form of identification
* Always tell someone where you are going
* Learn to apply the basic principles of first aid
* Reflective materials on your clothes or bike can save your life
* For safety on Mountains refer to the British Mountaineering Council publication *Safety on Mountains*
* Ride under control when going downhill, since this is often when serious accidents occur
* If you intend to ride fast off-road it is advisable to wear a helmet
* Particular care should be taken on unstable or wet surfaces

COMPETITIONS

* Events are organised by a number of clubs and national bodies. They can only take place with the permission of the landowner and/or highway authorities as appropriate.

FOLLOW THE COUNTRY CODE

* Enjoy the countryside and respect its life and work
* Guard against all risk of fire
* Fasten all gates
* Keep dogs under close control
* Keep to rights of way across farmland
* Use gates and stiles to cross fences, hedges and walls
* Leave livestock, crops and machinery alone
* Take your litter home
* Help to keep all water clean
* Protect wildlife, plants and trees
* Take special care of country roads
* Make no unnecessary noise

RICHARD PEACE is a freelance teacher and writer. He was educated at Queen Elizabeth Grammar School, Wakefield, and Magdalen College, Oxford, obtaining a degree in Modern History.

He now lives in Wakefield, West Yorkshire, and when not cycling or walking in England he travels and teaches abroad. His first book, YORKSHIRE DALES CYCLE WAY, is also available as a Hillside guide.

WEST YORKSHIRE CYCLE WAY

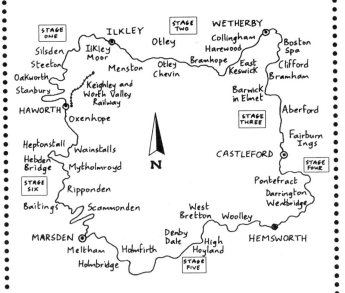